Uniclass

Uniclass

Unified Classification for the Construction Industry

RIBA Publications

Uniclass: Unified Classification for the Construction Industry
First edition 1997

Edited by Marshall Crawford, John Cann, Ruth O'Leary

© 1997
Construction Confederation
Royal Institute of British Architects
Royal Institution of Chartered Surveyors
Chartered Institution of Building Services Engineers
Department of the Environment Construction Sponsorship Directorate

Published by RIBA Publications, a division of RIBA Companies Ltd,
Finsbury Mission, 39 Moreland Street, London EC1V 8BB

ISBN 1 85946 031 3

Designed by Mike Stribbling, Gordon Burrows, Philip Handley

Typesetting by Mega Typesetting Limited, London

Printed by St Ives (Romford) Ltd

Illustration acknowledgement
Front Cover: Telegraph Colour Library

Contents

**Construction Project
Information Committee**

Construction Confederation
Royal Institute of British Architects
Royal Institution of Chartered Surveyors
Chartered Institution of Building Services Engineers
Institution of Civil Engineers

**Department of the
Environment**

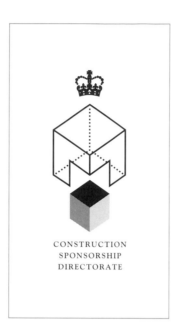

CONSTRUCTION
SPONSORSHIP
DIRECTORATE

Acknowledgements

Brief history

This three-year project to unify the classification systems in use in the UK has its roots in early work in CIB (International Council for Building Research Studies and Documentation) Commission W74 and, since 1988, in ISO TC59/SC13 Working Group 2. Tony Allott (RIBA Companies) and Henry Karlsson (Swedish Building Centre) were the co-authors of the original report which became ISO Technical Report 14177 *Classification of information in the construction industry* July 1994. The Technical Report is being used as the basis for an ISO Standard on classification of construction information which should be published in late 1997.

This classification scheme is based in part on at least four other important schemes: CI/SfB, CAWS (Common Arrangement of Work Sections for building works), CESMM3 (Civil Engineering Standard Method of Measurement, third edition) and EPIC (Electronic Product Information Co-operation). We are indebted to all the people who developed those schemes and to the many users whose comments helped us in integrating the various systems into a unified classification.

The work would not have been possible without the support and direction of the Unified Classification Steering Group:

Douglas Smith FRIBA, FLI, FRSA
Chairman, CPIC
Chairman of the Steering Group

Peter Jordan CEng, MICE, FCIOB
Secretary to CPIC

Ivan Dickason FCIOB
representing CC*

Keith Snook
representing RIBA

Joe Martin FRICS
representing RICS

David Russell CEng, FCIBSE
representing CIBSE

Ed Criswick
representing Department of the Environment Construction Sponsorship Directorate

Jonathan Gammon CEng
representing ICE

Drick Vernon
representing ICE

Annette O'Brien
representing CIIG

John Keenan
representing BSI

Uniclass project

The Uniclass project was funded by the sponsoring organisations (CC*, RIBA, RICS and CIBSE) with matching funds from the Department of the Environment Construction Sponsorship Directorate. We are grateful for the support given by these organisations to the project.

Many people helped in the production of this publication and we particularly wish to thank those who responded to the Consultative Documents and gave feedback at the public consultation meetings. The Construction Industry Information Group (CIIG) members have been particularly helpful in their comments.

A major contribution to this classification was provided by Dor Pontin who developed Table C, Management. She wishes to acknowledge her debt to the *London Classification of Business Studies*, ASLIB, 1979. The RIBA Plan of Work was also useful in developing the project management module of the table. Another source document of great importance was the CIB Master List, 1993 revised edition, which was the main source for Table N, Properties and characteristics.

The Uniclass project was led by Marshall Crawford supported by John Cann and Ruth O'Leary, all of NBS Services.

Peter Adderley provided editorial assistance during the preparation for publication as consultant to RIBA Publications.

*The Construction Confederation consists of the original members of the Building Employers Confederation (NFB, NCG, HBF, FBSC, BWF) together with the MCG, CECA and SBEF.

Acknowledgements

Biographies

Marshall Crawford BA, MLS, MIInfSc is the Information Services Director at NBS Services which he joined in August 1989. Marshall is active in the international working group for EPIC (Electronic Product Information Co-operation). At NBS he is responsible for the Technical Information Service which publishes (in a joint venture with Technical Indexes Ltd) standards and technical documents in both microfiche and CD-ROM formats.

John Cann MA(Cantab), PGDip has worked for NBS Services since 1994, where he has been involved in the international standardisation of classification of construction information with ISO TC59/SC13 Working Group 2, and has worked on electronic information storage/retrieval.

Ruth O'Leary BA(Hons), MSc, ALA, MIInfSc has worked for NBS Services since 1992, specialising in computer-based classification and retrieval, and is involved in the Electronic Product Information Co-operation.

Preface

New system

Uniclass is a new classification scheme for the construction industry, the full name of which is "Unified Classification for the Construction Industry". The Construction Industry Project Information Committee (CPIC), representing the four major sponsor organisations (the Construction Confederation, the Royal Institute of British Architects, the Royal Institution of Chartered Surveyors and the Chartered Institution of Building Services Engineers), and the Department of the Environment Construction Sponsorship Directorate were responsible for commissioning and steering the project, which was developed by NBS Services on behalf of CPIC.

Uniclass is a classification scheme for organising library materials and for structuring product literature and project information. It incorporates both CAWS (Common Arrangement of Work Sections for building works) and EPIC (Electronic Product Information Co-operation), a new system for structuring product data and product literature.

Structure

Uniclass follows the international framework set out in ISO Technical Report 14177 *Classification of information in the construction industry* July 1994, and builds upon the success of CAWS. It is also intended to supersede Cl/SfB, the most commonly used classification system for construction information. Cl/SfB was last revised in 1976, and when the question of its revision was reviewed by the SfB Agency in the UK it was decided that replacing it with a Unified Classification was the best solution. The main reasons for this were:

- International developments: the advance of computerisation and the limitations of SfB in this respect caused several countries to review their information structures and explore new concepts in information analysis. Through work in ISO, ICIS (International Construction Information Society) and EPIC, the UK was able to benefit from co-operative efforts in developing classification theory and practical tables.

- CAWS: the publication of CAWS in 1987 introduced an alternative information structuring scheme which became widely used through NBS (National Building Specification), SMM7 (Standard Method of Measurement of Building Works, seventh edition), and NES (National Engineering Specification). CAWS and Cl/SfB were operating in parallel, and one of the objectives of the Unified Classification project was to integrate CAWS into a new system.

- Currency: Cl/SfB did not reflect changes in the industry, including many new building types, concepts involving energy and environmental issues. The whole system needed updating for new topics.

- Notation: the brackets and the combinations of upper case and lower case letters made the codes difficult for users to understand. This complex notation also caused problems with computerisation.

The consultants would be glad to receive feedback on the implementation and use of the classification scheme and will maintain a record of enquiries and their follow-up. Please send queries and comments direct to:

Uniclass
NBS Services
Mansion House Chambers
The Close
Newcastle upon Tyne NE1 3RE
Telephone: (0191) 232 9594
Fax: (0191) 232 5714

Introduction

Uniclass is for use in organising many different forms of information including documents in libraries, project information, cost information, specifications, etc. Many potential users of Uniclass are at present users of CI/SfB and/or CAWS (Common Arrangement of Work Sections for building works). Uniclass includes all the topics covered by these two schemes, and in addition it presents some new tables and parts of tables, notably Table L Construction products, and a new project lifecycle classification (part of Table C Management).

Uniclass comprises 15 tables, each of which represents a different broad facet of construction information. Each table can be used as a "stand alone" table for the classification of a particular type of information, but, in addition, terms from different tables can be combined to classify complex subjects (see section on signs, below).

Many of the tables are inter-related in the sense that the same or similar words can appear in more than one table. For example "windows" appears in the Construction products table, in the Elements for buildings table and in the Work sections for buildings table. The difference is that in the Construction products table windows are off-the-shelf products; in the Elements table windows are parts of buildings; and in the Work sections table it is the process of installing windows and its result which are classified.

Below is a full list of tables in Uniclass, with a brief description of their important features. Definitions of the terms used and examples are given in the introductions to each of the tables.

A   Form of information
This table is useful for organising reference material in libraries, and also, when using combined codes, for denoting the medium in which information is published.

B   Subject disciplines
Uniclass tables are intended to be used by practitioners of any discipline within the construction industry; however, this table will be useful where it is appropriate to organise information according to subject discipline.

C   Management
This table has a similar basis to that of B, since it classifies management and project management as subject disciplines. The project management section is intended also for classifying project information according to the stage in the lifecycle of a project in which the information is generated.

D   Facilities
This table classifies construction works according to the user activity (or purpose) which they are intended to serve; the scale of the construction works is not explicitly given, so each code can equally well be used for classifying a complex, a construction entity (see below) or a space.

E   Construction entities
A construction entity is an independent construction of significant scale, e.g. a building, bridge, dam, etc. This table classifies construction entities according to physical form/basic function, as opposed to user activity which is covered by the Facilities table.

1 General *continued*

The table is to be used in two main ways: firstly to classify information on types of construction works which are not covered by the Facilities table; secondly as a qualifier to codes in the Facilities table to indicate the scale of a facility and the physical form/basic function of a facility. The Construction entities table can also be used to classify the scale of a construction works, i.e. whether it is a complex or an entity (see E0).

F   Spaces
This table classifies spaces according to a number of different characteristics including their location, scale, and degree of enclosure, but not according to user activity (see Table D Facilities). It is to be used in a similar way to Table E: firstly to classify information on types of spaces not covered by the Facilities table; secondly as a qualifier to codes in the Facilities table to indicate the scale of a facility (in this case, that the facility is a space).

G   Elements for buildings
This table classifies major physical parts of buildings and can be used for organising both design and cost information.

H   Elements for civil engineering works
This table uses the same main headings as the Construction entities table (with the exception of buildings and construction complexes). For each type of construction entity the table classifies the major functional parts. The primary use is expected to be for cost analysis.

J   Work sections for buildings
This table is based on the well known Common Arrangement of Work Sections for building works (CAWS), and incorporates changes to be made for the second edition of CAWS. It is used for organising information in specifications and bills of quantities and for classifying information on particular types of construction operation.

K   Work sections for civil engineering works
This table is based on CESMM3, and has similar uses to those of Table J.

L   Construction products
This table is based on Electronic Product Information Co-operation (EPIC), an international classification for construction products. It is used for classifying trade literature and design/technical information relating to construction products.

M   Construction aids
This table is for classifying trade literature and technical information relating to plant and equipment used for aiding construction operations.

N   Properties and characteristics
This table is for classifying information on subjects related to properties and characteristics (for example a book on fire safety); for the arrangement of information in technical documents; and for adding as a qualifier to codes from other tables.

P Materials
This table is for classifying different kinds of material, and also for adding as a qualifier to codes from other tables, especially the construction products table (for example classify aluminium framed windows at L413:P43).

Q Universal Decimal Classification (UDC)
This table indicates how UDC can be used to classify subjects not covered elsewhere in the Uniclass system. Only the main headings of UDC are given.

2 Technical description

2.1 Notation

Uniclass notation consists of a single capital letter followed by zero or more digits, except for the Work sections tables (Table J and Table K) which have two initial capital letters so as to incorporate the CAWS and CESMM3 codes. To allow easy shortening of the notation the numbers are not padded out with trailing zeros to create a fixed number of digits. This causes no problems for computerised sorting systems, but sometimes confuses people who may intuitively think that, for example, D11 files after D2 (see 2.3 Filing order, below).

The Uniclass notation is hierarchical; for example D21, D22, D23, etc. are always subclasses of D2. This means that if, for your purposes, you do not require the full detail of the Uniclass tables you can delete digits and classify at a higher level in the hierarchy. This allows Uniclass to be used in many different situations, with differing degrees of detail.

2.2 Signs

In the Uniclass system, three main signs are used to combine simple class numbers to create class numbers for complex subjects. These are the plus sign +, the slash sign /, and the colon sign : . There are also two specialist signs which are not intended for general use, the less-than sign < and the greater-than sign >. Uniclass signs are used in a similar way to their equivalents in UDC, with the exception of < and > which are not used in UDC.

The most used sign is likely to be the colon since this is the basic mechanism for combining facets (either from the same table or from different tables). It corresponds to the dividing lines of the four cell box in the CI/SfB system (└─┴─┴─┴─┘), but provides a simpler and more flexible way of combining class numbers, and is also compatible with computerised retrieval systems.

+
The plus sign is used to indicate a broad subject range of **non-consecutive** classes. For example, **D32+D52** means "Office facilities and entertainment facilities".

2 Technical description
continued

/

The slash sign is used to indicate a broad range of **consecutive** classes. For example, **D32/D34** means "Office facilities, commercial facilities and shops". Thus D32/D34 is equivalent to D32+D33+D34. In the Uniclass tables, codes combined with a slash sign are often presented in abbreviated form; for example, D32/D34 is presented as D32/4.

:

The colon sign is used to indicate "one construction object or subject in relation to another". For example, to represent the complex concept "Climate control system (HVAC) products for offices" one may combine the individual class numbers with the colon sign, giving **L75:D32**. Another example might be "Owner occupied residential flats", which may be represented by the combined class number **D8151:D8111**.

The colon sign does not specify which subject influences the other, nor does it show the nature of the influence exerted. Therefore the order of subjects does not affect the meaning of the combined class number (L75:D32 is the same as D32:L75). L75:D32 strictly means "Climate control system products *in relation to* offices", but in this case "Climate control system products *for* offices" is a sensible interpretation.

Two class numbers combined with a colon sign always represent a narrower subject than either of the class numbers on their own; this may be contrasted with the plus and the slash signs which always represent a broader subject.

<, >

The less-than and greater-than signs are used to indicate that one construction object is part of another. For example **D32<D41** means "An office facility which is part of a hospital"; and **G252<D32** means "Internal walls which are part of an office facility". The order of class numbers is important for this sign because **D41<D32** would mean "a medical facility which is part of an office".

In some cases it might be desired to file the information under the larger construction object, while preserving the meaning. To achieve this the order of the class numbers is changed and the **sign must also be changed** from a less-than sign to a greater-than sign; e.g. **D41>D32** still means "An office facility which is part of a hospital", but is now filed in the hospitals section rather than the offices section. In all cases the rule is that the open end of the sign must be adjacent to the number representing the larger object.

The less-than and greater-than signs are in effect specialised versions of the colon sign which attach a specific meaning to the relationship between the class numbers.

Please note that these signs have not been used explicitly in any of the Uniclass tables since they are only intended for use in specialist applications. In particular the Elements table contains combined codes indicating whole-part relationships for which these signs could be used, but colons are used instead to avoid the need for too many signs in general uses of Uniclass. In any case it is clear in the Elements table that, for example, a window is always part of a wall, and not vice versa.

2 Technical description
continued

The filing order of simple codes is as presented in the schedules: the initial letters are filed alphabetically; under each letter the first number is then considered and documents filed in numerical order according to this; then the second number is considered and so on. This means that, for example, D11 files before D2.

A useful aid when determining the filing order is to think of the numerical parts of the codes as following an imaginary decimal point. If this is done then the codes simply file in an ascending numerical order. For example, D11 files before D2 because 0.11 comes before 0.2 in an ascending numerical sequence.

The filing order of signs is given below; this is important when filing documents classified using combined codes.

+	e.g. D32+D52	Office and entertainment facilities
/	e.g. D32/D34	Office, commercial and trading facilities
simple number	e.g. D32	Office facilities
:	e.g. D32:E84	Intelligent office buildings
<	e.g. D32<D41	An office facility which is part of a hospital

This filing order for signs follows the rule "the general files before the specific".

The citation order is the order in which codes are cited when assigning a combined class number. For example, do we assign the code D32:E84 or the code E84:D32 to the subject Intelligent office buildings? The two orders of code both mean the same thing, but one will have to be chosen as the main number at which, for example, a book is filed on a shelf.

The default Uniclass citation order is the same as the filing order, that is in the above example we would use the code D32:E84. However, it is still possible for users of Uniclass to set their own citation order for particular uses, provided they are not concerned about the exact compatibility of the codes they assign with codes that someone else in another organisation assigns.

In the Uniclass system different scales/complexities of construction works are recognised. In order of decreasing scale/complexity these are: construction complexes, construction entities, spaces, elements.

In many cases it will not be necessary to distinguish between construction complexes and construction entities; for example, both office complex and office building may be classified at D32. However, if it is necessary to make this distinction of scale, then the appropriate class number from Table E Construction entities may be combined using a colon with the D32, thus: D32:E0 Office complex; D32:E8 Office building.

Introduction

Similarly, if it is necessary to indicate that the construction object in question is a space rather than a complex or a building, the class number from the facilities table may be combined using a colon with the class number from the Spaces table – for example: D32:F Office space; D32:F2 Office room.

However, colons should only be used as indicated above when absolutely necessary. It is not necessary to use combined class numbers when:

(a) user activity is of prime importance in your collection and the distinction between construction complexes, entities and spaces is of little importance;

(b) entries in the Facilities table themselves imply a particular size/complexity. For example D412 District general hospitals – these are nearly always construction complexes and certainly are never spaces in another building. Therefore in this case it is sufficient to use the class number D412; using D412:E0 would amount to tautology.

3 Layout of codes in the tables

The following diagram shows the typical layout of codes in a Uniclass table. An important point is that the sub-headings only include the last digit of the Uniclass code which applies to them and there may be up to three levels of sub-heading. This example shows two levels of sub-heading – when assigning a Uniclass code to a level 2 sub-heading you must take the code for the standard heading, add the digit for the

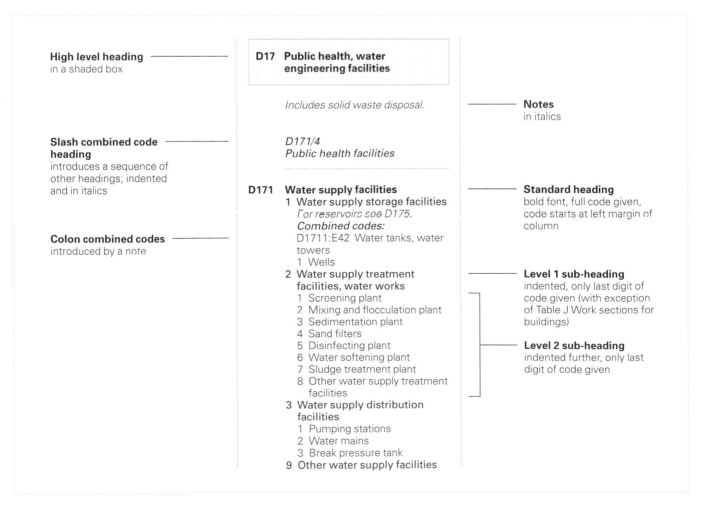

High level heading
in a shaded box

D17 Public health, water engineering facilities

Includes solid waste disposal. ———— **Notes**
in italics

Slash combined code heading
introduces a sequence of other headings; indented and in italics

D171/4
Public health facilities

D171 Water supply facilities
  1 Water supply storage facilities
    For reservoirs see D175.
    Combined codes:
    D1711:E42 Water tanks, water towers
    1 Wells
  2 Water supply treatment facilities, water works
    1 Screening plant
    2 Mixing and flocculation plant
    3 Sedimentation plant
    4 Sand filters
    5 Disinfecting plant
    6 Water softening plant
    7 Sludge treatment plant
    8 Other water supply treatment facilities
  3 Water supply distribution facilities
    1 Pumping stations
    2 Water mains
    3 Break pressure tank
  9 Other water supply facilities

Colon combined codes
introduced by a note

———— **Standard heading**
bold font, full code given, code starts at left margin of column

———— **Level 1 sub-heading**
indented, only last digit of code given (with exception of Table J Work sections for buildings)

———— **Level 2 sub-heading**
indented further, only last digit of code given

level 1 sub-heading, and then add the digit for the level 2 sub-heading. For example, the Uniclass code for Water mains is D17132. However, it is important to only use the level of detail appropriate for your needs when assigning Uniclass codes (see section 4, below); so, for example, you may wish to classify water mains at D1713 or D171.

4 Using Uniclass to classify documents

It is important to use Uniclass at the simplest level appropriate for your needs.

4.1 Simple use for a small collection of similar material

At the most simple level you can use just a single Uniclass table without any combined codes, and use only the level of detail given in the concise version of the table. For example, you might have a small collection of trade literature describing construction products. The most appropriate table to use in this case is the Construction products table (Table L). A single code from the Construction products concise table should be assigned to each item of literature. In order to decide the correct code, it may be necessary to refer to the Index and the Construction products full table, but it will not be necessary to use the long codes given in the full table: these can be shortened to the corresponding code given in the concise table. For example, if you have an item of trade literature on windows, you would consult the index, see that windows are classified at L413, then go to the concise Construction products table. Here the longest codes consist of an L and two digits, so to arrive at the concise code from the long code given in the index simply remove digits from the end of the long code until there are only two remaining. In this case this gives us L41, which is therefore the concise code for Window products.

4.2 Extending the simple use

If your collection of trade literature is larger you may wish to extend the simple use in one or more of a number of ways. You could:
- use the long codes given in the Construction products full table;
- use codes from the Materials table as qualifiers where necessary. For example aluminium windows could be classified as L413:P43;
- use codes from more than one table as qualifiers. For example codes from both the Facilities table and the Materials table could be used as qualifiers where necessary, so that, as well as the above example for aluminium windows, you could classify floor tiles for swimming pools as L5331:D54.

4.3 Classifying a small but complex collection with single codes

Another possibility is that your collection is complex, containing documents of different types. For example, as well as trade literature you might have reference books on a number of different subjects, British Standards, documents explaining regulations and cost information on different types of facilities. However, for a small collection you are likely to want to avoid the complication of combined codes and simply assign a single code from a particular table to each document.

4 Using Uniclass to classify documents *continued*

The procedure for classifying a document will then be:

- Which table is the document best classified by? For example: the trade literature is likely to be best classified by the Construction products table (Table L); the reference books are likely to be best classified according to Subject discipline (Table B); the British Standards and the documents explaining regulations are likely to best be classified by Table A (with the standards arranged numerically according to BS number, and the explanatory documents arranged alphabetically); and cost information is likely to be best classified by the Facilities table (Table D).
- Which code from that table is the relevant one for this document? It is likely that a short code from the concise version of the table will be sufficient.

4.4 Classifying a large, complex collection using combined codes

For large, complex collections, it may be useful to combine codes from more than one table (and/or a number of codes from a single table) to classify the concepts contained in a document or other piece of information. The procedure for classifying a document in this case will be:

- What are the concepts contained in the document?
- Which table do we use to classify each concept?
- How do we combine the codes? In other words, what sign do we use between codes, and what citation order do we use (see sections 2.2 and 2.4, above)?

5 Retrieving information classified by Uniclass

To retrieve information classified by Uniclass:

- look in the Uniclass index for the word which describes your query;
- go to the place in the Uniclass tables to which you are referred;
- check that the context is correct and that there is not another position in Uniclass which better describes what you are looking for;
- go to the point in the classified collection of information which corresponds to your Uniclass code, remembering the Uniclass filing order (see section 2.3, above).

N.B. If you are trying to retrieve a colon combined code, remember that either component of the code could come first, so you need to find out what citation order has been used to classify the collection (see section 2.4, above); if this is not clear, you may need to check in both possible locations.

6 Use of Uniclass with computerised information

6.1 Classifying computerised information according to Uniclass

Uniclass is compatible with information held on computerised databases, and any existing database can simply have a field added to accept the Uniclass code; see for example Figure 1 which shows a form used as a front end for a library database created using Microsoft Access. Codes for each item in the database can be assigned using this manual and then added to the database. Simple Uniclass codes will automatically sort in the correct Uniclass filing order.

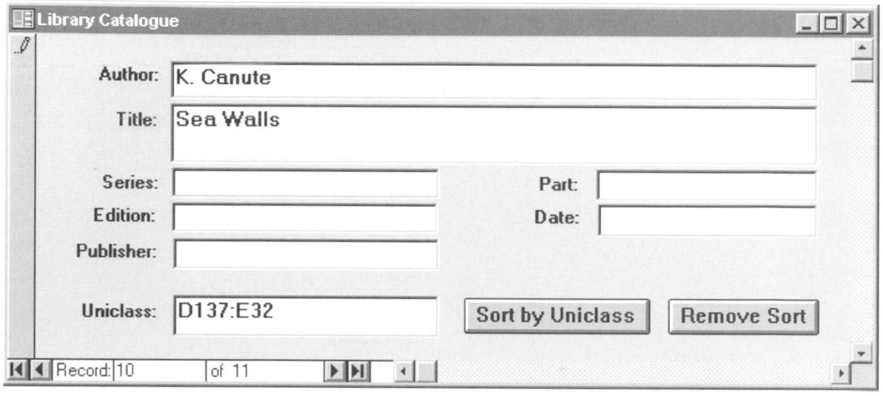

Figure 1
Example of a form for a library catalogue database, including a button which runs a macro to sort the records in Uniclass filing order.

6.2 Technical information on sorting combined codes in the correct Uniclass filing order in a computerised database

To get combined codes to sort in the correct Uniclass filing order, the sort must be carried out on a calculated field equal to the Uniclass code with a colon added on to the end of it. When using Microsoft Access this is achieved by creating a query which sorts on the expression [Uniclass] & ":", where [Uniclass] represents the field containing the Uniclass codes, and the ampersand is the symbol used for combining text strings (see Figure 3). The form in Figure 1 can be directly based on the query, in which case it will automatically sort the records in Uniclass order every time it is opened; alternatively, if another sort order is required as the default, then the Uniclass sort order can be applied when required by adding a command button to the form which when clicked runs a macro (see Figure 2) that applies the query as a filter to the form.

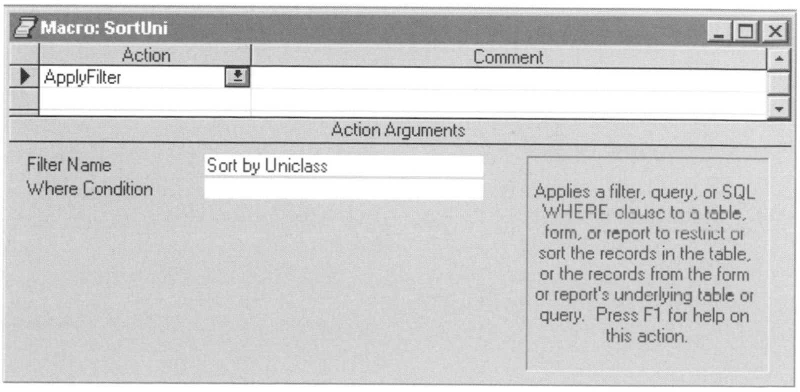

Figure 2
The design of the macro which is run when the 'Sort by Uniclass' button is clicked. The filter name 'Sort by Uniclass' is the name of the query shown in Figure 3.

Figure 3
The design of the query which is applied as a filter to the form in Figure 1 when the 'Sort by Uniclass' button is clicked. Both QBE grid (top) and SQL code (bottom) are given. The term '[LIBRARY CATALOGUE].*' stands for all the fields in the table named LIBRARY CATALOGUE on which the query is based.

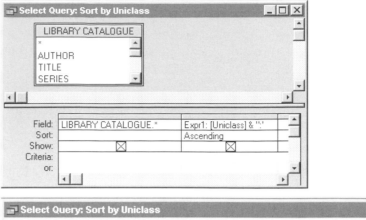

6.3 Retrieving computerised information classified according to Uniclass

The method of retrieving computerised information classified according to Uniclass depends to a certain extent on the search tools which the manager of the database has set up to help you achieve this. However, first you need to find the correct Uniclass code which covers your query, in a similar way to that outlined in section 5, above. Then you can use that code as a search term. However, it is very helpful if the search tool you are using supports front and back truncation, because this enables you to do a broad search to begin with and then limit the records retrieved if necessary. Also it will enable you to find relevant codes whether or not they have been combined with other codes using colons. For example, if you want to search for information on retaining /protecting walls, it is useful to be able to search for *E32* where * is a wildcard character. This enables you to retrieve information on sea walls classified at D137:E32 plus more precise information on retaining walls classified at E321.

Form of information

A

Definition

The description "Form of information" encompasses a number of related features of information including: the style of presentation of the information (such as dictionary, guide, etc.); the basic nature or status of the information (such as legislation, standards, etc.); and the type of medium on which the information is stored (such as book, leaflet, CD-ROM, microfiche). This table does not classify the subject matter of documents.

Examples

Book, journal, leaflet, CD-ROM, microfiche, standards, legislation, dictionaries.

Use

This table may be used on its own for organising general reference information (dictionaries, telephone directories, legislation, standards) where the subject coverage is extremely broad and it would be difficult to classify the material into one of the more detailed tables which follow Table A. It may also be used in combination with other tables to indicate both form and subject, for example: D56:A14 Surveys of sports facilities.

A1 General reference works

A11 Dictionaries, encyclopedias
1 Dictionaries
2 Encyclopedias

A12 Guides, directories
1 Guides
2 Directories

A13 Catalogues

A14 Surveys

A15 Statistics

A16 Price books

A17 Learning materials, textbooks

A18 Reports

A19 Other

A2 Legislation, legal documents

See also B91 Law.
Includes regulatory documents
and explanatory documents.
Excludes standards (see A3).

A21/3
UK legislation

A21 Primary legislation (Acts of Parliament)

A22 Secondary legislation
1 Statutory Instruments, etc.
Includes the Building Regulations and the CDM Regulations, but see also C506 Health and safety plan.
2 Bylaws

A23 Quasi-legislation (also called tertiary legislation)
e.g. approved codes of practice, circulars, policy guidance.
Subdivide alphabetically.

A24 International, European legislation

A25 Case law reports
Combined codes:
A25:B5 Planning case law reports

A26 Patents, licences, copyright
Includes intellectual property rights (IPR).
1 Patents
2 Licences
3 Copyright

A29 Other legislation, legal documents

A3 National and international standards

Includes explanatory documents/guides.

A31 British Standards

A32 European Standards

A33 ISO Standards

A34 De facto standards

A39 Other

A4 Other rules, recommendations

e.g. those published by specialist industry bodies.

A5 Standard specifications

e.g. NBS, NES. Includes explanatory documents/guides.

A6 Standard contracts

Includes certificates and administration forms (unless in C72). Includes explanatory documents/guides.
See also C71 Construction preparation/project planning and C72 Construction operations on site.

A9 Types of medium

A91 Books

A92 Journals

A93 Pamphlets, leaflets, unbound printed material

A94 Drawings

A95 Photographic information

A96 Microfiche, microfilm

A97 Video, film

A98 Media accessed via a computer
1 Optical discs, CD-ROM, DVD
2 Magnetic disks, floppy disks
3 Magnetic tape
4 Online information, Internet information

A99 Other special forms of information
1 Models
Includes architects' models.

Subject disciplines

B

Definition	"Subject discipline" refers to the body of knowledge which is centred on a profession or field of knowledge.
Examples	Architecture, engineering, surveying, contracting, town and country planning.
Use	This table may be used for classifying reference material which is related to the theory (such as structural engineering) or history (such as periods or styles of architecture) or other general aspects of a discipline. Information relating to a specific stage in the project lifecycle should be classified by Table C. *For Management as a discipline see Table C.*

Subject disciplines

B

For a more complete list of agents in the construction industry see C38.
For management as a discipline see Table C.
For project management see C5/C9.
For facilities management see C81.

B1 Architecture

B11 Architecture by name of architect

B12 Architecture by geographical region, guidebooks

B13 History of architecture, periods and styles of architecture

B14 Architectural design (excluding structural design), spatial design
For structural design see B25.

B15 Interior design, decoration

B16 Landscape architecture

B2 Engineering

Combined codes:
B2:D15 Communications engineering
B2:D17 Public health engineering

B21 Engineering by name of engineer

B22 Engineering by geographical region

B23 History of engineering

B24 Civil engineering, general

B25 Structural engineering, structural design
For spatial design see B14.

B26 Services engineering
1 Building services engineering
2 Mechanical engineering
Other than building services.
3 Electrical engineering
Other than building services.

B27 Other engineering

B3 Surveying

B31 Quantity surveying, cost analysis

B32 Building surveying

B33 Site surveying, land surveying

B4 Contracting, building

B5 Town and country planning

To classify planning for a particular end-use, combine with codes from the Facilities or Construction entities tables, as follows:
B5:A25 Planning case law reports
B5:B91 Planning law
B5:D11/D14 Transport planning
B5:D137 Coastal planning
B5:D15 Telecommunications planning
B5:D16 Planning for power supply, mineral supply
B5:D17 Waste management, pollution control planning
B5:D261 Trees and forestry planning
B5:D34 Retail planning
B5:D4 Health care planning
B5:D5 Recreational planning
B5:D8 Housing planning
B5:E7 Planning for pipelines etc.

B50 History and theory of planning

B51 Planning control

B52 Planning policy guidance (ppg)

B53 Regional planning

B54 Development plans
Includes local plans, structure plans.

B55 Rural planning

B56 Urban planning

B57 Environmental planning
1 Environmental assessment
2 Environmental protection
3 Contaminated land
4 Sites of Special Scientific Interest (SSSI)

B58 Conservation
1 Conservation areas
2 Historic buildings
3 Ancient monuments
4 Archaeological areas

B59 Other kinds of planning
1 Planning for gypsies, travellers

B7 Other construction-related disciplines

For a more complete list of agents in the construction industry see C38.
For project management see C5/C9.
For facilities management see C81.

B71 GIS (Geographical Information System) engineering

B9 Other disciplines

B91 Law
See also A2 Legislation, legal documents.
Combined codes:
B91:B5 Planning law
1 International law, EU law
2 National law
3 Financial law including taxation
4 Criminal law
5 Civil law
6 Legal practice and procedure
 1 National, EU, etc. practice and procedure
 2 Public inquiries, appeals
 3 Dispute procedures
7 Legal professional responsibilities and roles
Includes legal aspects of partnerships, professional insurance/liability, warranties, negligence claims, roles of expert witnesses

B92 Science/technology

B93 Computing, information technology
For management of computing, information technology see C46.
1 Computer hardware
2 Computer software
3 Computer applications
 1 Networking, intranet
 2 E-mail
 3 Internet, World Wide Web

27

B Subject disciplines

B94 **Behavioural sciences**

B95 **Communication**
Of information and ideas generally.

B96 **Political science**

B97 **Information science**

Management

C

Definition

Processes with the purpose of planning, administrating or assessing, with particular reference to the construction industry and its agents.

Examples

Management theory, corporate strategy, marketing, risk analysis, project management.

Use

Information concerning all aspects of management, whether relating to the construction industry at large, the operation of a company or practice, project management, or a particular stage in the life-cycle of a construction project.

Concise Table

C1 Management theory, systems and activities

C11 Corporate strategy
C12 Quality management
C13 Security, industrial espionage, trade secrets
C14 Objective setting
C15 Decision making
C16 Problem solving
C17 Co-ordination
C18 Appraisal, assessment
C19 Other

C2 Management personnel

C21 Top management, directors, partners
C22 Other levels of management

C3 Type of business/organisation

C31 Organisations by scale and location
C32 Private enterprises
C33 Mixed enterprises and partnerships
C34 Government and related organisations
C35 Public enterprises
C36 Non-profit-making organisations, charities
C37 Industrial and commercial associations
C38 Construction industry
C39 Other types of organisation

C4 Specialist areas of management

C41 Management of office services
C42 Marketing, selling
C43 Research and development
C44 Finance and accounting, business economics
C45 Personnel management and industrial relations
C46 Management of computing, information technology

C5/C9 Management of construction activities/project management

C50 General techniques/information

C61 Inception/procurement
C62 Feasibility
C63 Outline proposals/programme preparation
C64 Scheme design/costing
C65 Detail design/costing
C66 Production information
C67 Bills of quantities
C68 Tender action

C71 Construction preparation/project planning
C72 Construction operations on site
C73 Completion

C81 Occupation/facilities management
C83 Feedback
C84 Refurbishment and recommissioning

C91 Decommissioning
C92 Demolition etc.
C93 Redevelopment

Management

C1 Management theory, systems and activities

C11 Corporate strategy

C111 Corporate policy, mission statements

C112 Corporate planning

C113 Corporate development

C12 Quality management

C121 Total quality management (TQM)

C122 Management control

C123 Quality assurance

C13 Security, industrial espionage, trade secrets

C14 Objective setting

C15 Decision making

C16 Problem solving

C17 Co-ordination

C18 Appraisal, assessment

C181 SWOT analysis
SWOT = Strengths, Weaknesses, Opportunities, Threats

C19 Other

C191 Delegation of authority

C192 Ethics, responsibility, conduct
See also C4224 Marketing ethics.

C193 Awards
For Competitions see C613.

C2 Management personnel

C21 Top management, directors, partners

C211 President

C212 Chairman

C213 Chief executive

C214 Managing director

C215 Partner

C216 Other executive director

C217 Non-executive director

C22 Other levels of management

C3 Type of business/ organisation

C31 Organisations by scale and location

C311 International, multinational

C312 European

C313 UK

C314 National organisations operating in countries other than the UK

C315 Regional organisations

C316 Local organisations

C32 Private enterprises

C321 Sole ownerships
i.e. sole traders, one-man practices.

C322 Partnerships

C323 Professional firms, consultants
For construction industry consultants see C38.

C324 Limited companies

C325 Joint stock companies
Includes private and public companies, holding companies, etc.

C326 Co-operative associations
i.e. associations of consumers or producers engaged in trade, who share out profits among their members.

C327 Conglomerate companies
i.e. companies engaged in several industries.

C328 Business consortia
i.e. groups of companies associated together for a particular purpose, including joint ventures.

C329 Agencies

C33 Mixed enterprises and partnerships

C331 Mixed enterprises
i.e. firms which are partly privately and partly government held.

C332 Public/private partnerships
i.e. partnerships involving separate organisations, one or more owned by the government, and one or more owned privately. An example of this type of partnership would be one involved in a PFI (Private Finance Initiative) scheme.

C34 Government and related organisations

C341 Central government
Includes Ministries, Departments.

C342 Local government
1 Professional departments within local government
  1 Local authority architects
  2 Local authority engineers
  3 Local authority surveyors
  4 Local authority planners
2 Direct works organisations

C35 Public enterprises

C351 Nationalised firms

C352 Public corporations

C353 State enterprises

C354 The armed forces

C355 Civil service

C356 Police service

C359 Other

C36 Non-profit-making organisations, charities

C37 Industrial and commercial associations

C371 Trade associations

C372 Research organisations

C373 Employers associations

C374 Professional associations

C375 Special interest groups

C376 Trade unions

C38 Construction industry

See Table B for information concerning subject disciplines, as distinct from types of organisation.

C381 General
1 General (non-discipline-related)

C382 Clients, managers
1 Clients
2 Project managers
3 Facilities managers

C383 Architectural/general designers/consultants
1 Architects
2 Interior designers
3 Landscape architects
4 Building surveyors
Includes party wall surveyors.
9 Other

C384 Civil/structural engineering designers/consultants
1 Structural engineers
2 Road engineers
3 Maritime engineers
4 Water engineers
9 Other

C385 Services engineering designers/consultants
1 Electrical engineers
Other than general services engineers.
2 Telecommunications engineers
3 Mechanical engineers
Other than general services engineers.
  1 Heating and ventilation engineers
4 Public health engineers
5 Acoustic engineers
9 Other

C386 Other technical consultants
1 Town and country planners
2 Building control officers
Includes approved inspectors.
3 Geographic information system (GIS) engineers and land surveyors
4 Quantity surveyors, cost engineers
5 Health/safety/ environmental consultants
Includes planning supervisors.
6 Transportation planners
7 Design audit consultants
9 Other

C387 Legal/financial/management consultants
1 Legal consultants
2 Financial/leasing consultants
3 Insurance consultants
4 Management consultants
9 Other

C388 Contractors
1 Contractors
2 Sub-contractors

C389 Manufacturers, suppliers, other
1 Manufacturers
2 Distributors/suppliers
3 Importers
9 Other

C39 Other types of organisation

C391 Industries other than construction

C392 Temporary organisations

C393 Miscellaneous organisations
i.e. organisations not specifically listed in section C3.

C394 Small businesses

C395 Large businesses

C4 Specialist areas of management

For contract office services, outsourcing of office services see C813.

C41 Management of office services

For information technology, computing see C46.

C411 Switchboard services

C412 Reception services

C413 Commissionaire, security services

C414 Secretarial services

C415 Mail management

C416 Reprography
1 Photocopying, duplicating
2 Printing

C417 Records management
1 Control of office documents, collating, filing
2 Stationery, forms
3 Office library management and operations

C419 Other

C42 Marketing, selling

C421 General marketing activities
1 Marketing research, survey techniques
2 Audit/assessment
For financial audits see C4434.
3 Forecasting
4 Strategy establishment
i.e. the establishment of overall marketing strategy.
5 Policy making/operation
i.e. the development and operation of particular policies.

C422 Marketing concepts and systems
1 The marketing mix
2 Marketing models
3 Marketing information systems
4 Marketing ethics
See also C192 Ethics for general management ethics.

C423 Promotion
1 Advertising
2 Publicity
3 Public relations
4 Exhibitions of work
5 Media planning
6 Press releases
7 Promotional publications
8 Presentations
9 Workshops, seminars, conferences

C424 Sales management, selling
1 Target setting
2 Sales reporting systems

C425 Social marketing
i.e. marketing for motives other than profit.

C426 International marketing
1 Export marketing
2 Franchising

C427 Marketing by type of product

C43 Research and development

Includes research and development in general. For research organisations see C372.

C431 Research

C432 Testing

C433 Development

C434 Results of research
For patents see A261; for copyright see A263.
1 Inventions
2 Publication of research results

C44 Finance and accounting, business economics

C441 Financial world
1 Financial markets
2 Financial institutions
  1 Banks and banking
  2 Finance corporations
  3 Trusts

C442 Financial management
1 Asset management
  1 Capital raising methods
    For project funding see C4444 Funding.
  2 Leasing
  3 Debt financing
  4 Trading capital
  5 Credit management
  6 Licensing
  7 Investment project appraisal
    1 Overseas investment
  8 Liquid assets
  9 Financial risk analysis, others
2 Portfolio investment
  Includes investment in and management of securities.
3 Business formation and liquidation
  1 Setting up
  2 Mergers
  3 Flotations
  4 Partnering
  5 Asset swapping
  6 Divestment
  7 Liquidations
  8 Insolvencies
4 Land and property finance/development
  For premises property strategy see C811.
  1 Land and real estate
    Includes estate agency and valuation.
  2 Property finance
5 Personal financial management
  Includes personal saving, investment.

C443 Accounting and auditing
1 Accounting procedures
  1 Goodwill accounting
  2 Inflation accounting
  3 Accounting valuations
  4 Book-keeping systems
2 Management accounting
  1 Budgets
  2 Budgetary control
  3 Cost accounting
  4 Costs
    1 Fixed costs
    2 Variable costs
    3 Historical costs
    4 Job costing, timesheets
3 Accounting for external appraisal
  Includes annual accounts, accounting to shareholders.
4 Auditing
  For marketing audits see C4212.

C444 Business economics
1 History and theories of economics
2 Microeconomics
  1 Income
  2 Interest rates
  3 Profitability
  4 Productivity
3 Macroeconomics
  1 Investment and growth
    1 Economic aspects of the environment
      i.e. energy resources, land/mineral resources.
  2 Economic cycles
    1 Recession
    2 Boom
    3 Steady growth
    4 Flat
  3 Inflation and deflation
    1 Inflation
    2 Deflation
  4 Monetary economics
    1 Foreign exchange
    2 Exchange rates
    3 World banks
    4 International Monetary Fund
  5 Government economics
    1 Public finance, monetary policies
    2 National budget
    3 Government expenditure
      For grants, subsidies and funding see C44441.
    4 Government fund-raising, taxation
  6 Local government economics
    1 Rates, council taxes
4 Funding
  1 Government funding
    1 European Union
    2 National government
    3 Joint government/private sector funding
      e.g. Private Finance Initiative (PFI).
    4 National Lottery funding
    5 Local government grants, subsidies
  2 Private sector funding

C45 Personnel management and industrial relations

C451 Personnel management theory and systems
1 Personnel administration
2 Industrial psychology
3 Personnel policy
4 Personnel planning
5 Human resources development
6 Personnel records and systems

C452 Recruitment and selection
1 Job descriptions, requirements and enrichments
2 Educational qualifications, experience, skills
3 Applications, references
4 Interviews, tests
5 Selection, selection boards
6 Induction
7 Probationary period
8 Placement
9 Equal opportunities, discrimination

C453 Training
1 External training
  Includes schools of architecture, universities.
2 Internal training
  Includes apprenticeships, work experience, external placement experience.
3 Continuing professional development
4 Retraining

C454 Employee communication
For quality assurance manuals see C123.
1 Handbooks
2 Procedure manuals
3 House journals
4 Suggestion schemes
5 Consultation

C455 Industrial relations
1 Labour relations
2 Industrial democracy
3 Conciliation, arbitration
4 Co-partnerships
5 Worker control

C456 Conditions of employment
1 Hours of work
2 Breaks
3 Leave, absence
4 Conduct, disciplinary action
5 Dispute resolution
6 Termination of employment

C457 Remuneration
1 Salaries, wages
2 Compensation
3 Systems of payment
4 Incentives
5 Bonuses
7 Allowances
8 Deductions

C458 Working conditions, nature of work
For physical working conditions, working environment see C81 Occupation, facilities management.
For health and safety at work see C8159.
1 Dangerous work
2 Monotonous work

C459 Other personnel management issues
1 Fringe benefits
  1 Pensions
  2 Insurance
  3 Maternity benefits
  4 Sick pay
  5 Grants, loans, discount schemes to employees
2 Social benefits
See also C814 Premises services.
  1 Subsidised meals
  2 Vouchers
  3 Employees' housing
3 Status of personnel, promotion
4 Resource management
Includes office productivity, team structures.
5 Supervision
6 Employee appraisal
7 Job evaluation

C46 Management of computing, information technology

For computing, information technology in general see B93.

C461 Computer management strategy

C5/C9 Management of construction activities/project management

C50 General techniques/ information

C501 Programming

C502 Critical path analysis

C503 Monitoring techniques

C504 Methods of communication

C505 Risk analysis and management

C506 Health and safety plan
May include: details of parties involved, description of project, description of the existing environment, hazard assessments, implementation.

See C8159 for health and safety at work.
See C733 for health and safety file. For reference copies of CDM Regulations see A221, but if just Table C is being used CDM Regulations may be classified here.

C507 Quality plans

C508 Plans of work

C509 Job manuals

C61 Inception/procurement

C611 Client/contractor relationship
1 Conventional lump sum contracting
2 Design and build
3 Management contracting
4 Construction management

C612 Briefing by client

C613 Competition entries, competitions
For awards see C193

C614 Proposals

C615 Appointment of lead and other consultants
See C38 for types of consultant.
1 Compulsory competitive tendering

C62 Feasibility

C621 Appraisals
Includes option appraisals, project appraisals, feasibility studies.

C622 Surveys and structural implications of site

C623 Energy strategies
Includes services implications.

C624 Community and tenant liaison

C63 Outline proposals/programme preparation

C631 Outline proposals
1 Report and sketch plans
2 Cost models and indicative costs
3 Energy targets

C632 Programme preparation
1 Development control plan
2 Management control plan

C64 Scheme design/costing

C641 Completion of brief
1 Coordination of design development

C642 Full design of project

C643 Preliminary design

C644 Costing of design

C645 Submission of proposals for all approvals
Includes planning applications, building control, etc.

C65   Detail design/costing

Library materials: information on drawing equipment, drawing techniques and practice.

C651   Full design of every part and component

C652   Working drawings including CAD

C653   Completion of cost checking of designs, final cost plan

C66   Production information

C661   Production drawings

C662   Production schedules

C663   Production specifications

C67   Bills of quantities

C671   Bills of quantities

C672   Tender documents

C68   Tender action

C681   Drawing up list of tenderers

C682   Preliminary enquiries for invitation to tender

C683   Drawing up of shortlist and notification to tenderers

C684   Dispatch of tender documents

C685   Assessment of tenders and notification to tenderers

C686   Examination of priced bills

C687   Negotiated reduction of tenders

C71   Construction preparation/ project planning

For reference copies of standard contracts see A6, but if just Table C is being used standard contracts may be classified here.

C711   Contract documents
1 Compilation
2 Novation
3 Checking
4 Signature

C712   Insurance

C713   Site programme
1 Agreement of critical dates
2 Agree methods of progressing

C714   Project meetings
1 Arrangements for issuing instructions
2 Location, frequency and other arrangements for site meetings

C715   Contractor's pre-contract planning
1 Programming
2 Site layout
3 Liaison with engineers

C716   Tenant decanting

C72   Construction operations on site

*Includes management of construction operations.
For reference copies of certificates and administration forms see A6, but if just Table C is being used certificates and administration forms may be classified here.*

C721   Quality control
1 Quality control and management
2 Site inspection by consultants
3 Site inspection by clerk of works
4 Commissioning and testing

C722   Time control
1 Maintenance of programme
2 Claims for extension of time

C723   Cost control
1 Procedures for cost control
Includes claims for reimbursable costs, interim certificates and payments.

C724   Recording
1 Site meetings
2 Daywork records
3 Progress photographs

C73   Completion

C731   Detailed pre-completion inspection by consultants, contractor and sub-contractors

*C732/5
Hand-over/practical completion*

C732   Hand-over to client

C733   Health and safety file/operation and maintenance manual/ tenants' handbook
May include: project working drawings and as-built drawings; operation and maintenance manuals; description of possible hazards; historic site data; pre- and post-construction site survey information and other data; photographs of site elements, proving/load test results; commissioning test results; specification and description of in-built safety systems.

C734   Miscellaneous hand-over/ practical completion issues
1 Training of operating and maintenance staff
2 Tenant communications

C735   Certificate of practical completion

C736   Defects

C737   Final inspection

C738   Certificate of making good defects

C739   Final accounts/final certificate

C81   Occupation/facilities management

Includes control and organisation of the premises and its occupation, i.e. property strategy, space management, office services, premises services, maintenance, relocation.

C811   Property/premises strategy, planning and management
For land and property finance/development see C4424.
1 Performance analysis
2 Property and asset registers

C812 Space management
1 Space planning
2 Space design
3 Space standards
   Includes New Metric Handbook.
4 Accommodation, layouts
5 Mobile desking
6 Home working/teleworking

C813 Contract office services, outsourcing of office services
For general management of office services see C41.

C814 Premises services
1 Catering
2 Recreation
3 Nurseries
4 Crèches
5 Transport facilities
   Includes company cars.
6 Communication services
   Includes mobile phones.

C815 Maintenance and operation
Includes building and engineering maintenance.
1 Maintenance of external fabric of buildings or other structures
   Includes cleaning of external fabric, window cleaning.
2 Maintenance of internal fabric of buildings, decorating
3 Cleaning of interior of buildings
4 Operation and maintenance of building services
6 Energy management
7 Environmental strategies
   Includes environmental audits, lighting and colour, noise, temperature, comfort and amenities, dust control.
8 Life cycle costing
9 Health and safety at work
   For health and safety during construction, CDM, see C506.

C816 Emergency procedures
For risk analysis and management see C505.
1 Policies
2 Disaster recovery strategies
3 Fire strategies
4 Security strategies

C817 Relocation management
i.e. managing moves and changes.

C83 Feedback

C831 Analysis of job records

C832 Inspection of building

C833 Studies of building in use

C84 Refurbishment and recommissioning

C91 Decommissioning

C92 Demolition etc.

C921 Dismantling

C922 Demolition

C923 Disposal

C93 Redevelopment

Facilities

Definition

A facility is a construction complex, construction entity or space serving one or more user activity/purpose. A facility is identified by this user activity/purpose.

Related definitions
Construction entity: an independent construction of significant scale, e.g. a single building, bridge, road or dam.
Construction complex: two or more adjacent construction entities, collectively serving one or more user activity/purpose, e.g. an airport or an out of town shopping centre.
Space: an area or volume contained within, or otherwise associated with, a building or other construction entity, e.g. a room. A space may be bounded physically or notionally.

Examples of facilities

Hospital, prison, office, library, library study area.

Use

This table classifies construction works according to user activity, and can be used to organise building regulations, design requirements, historical information on design and costs, and information for property management.

Because the Facilities table classifies construction works according to user activity, it may also be used to classify the user activities themselves. For example the code D54 (Swimming facilities) can also be used to classify the activity of Swimming. However, if you need to clearly specify that you are classifying an activity, not a facility, then the code N41 should be added using a colon sign to the code D54 (giving D54:N41 or N41:D54), as indicated at section N41 in the Properties and characteristics table.

To classify mixed use developments, combine the codes for each of the individual uses; alternatively, if all the uses are in one particular main section, classify at the code for that main section.

N.B. If the uses appear sequentially in the schedules, use the / sign; otherwise use the + sign. For example:
- A mixed development of offices, commercial facilities and shops D32/D34; alternatively, classify at D3.
- A mixed development of offices and sports facilities D32+D56.

continued

D   Facilities

Notes

The Facilities table is based on Table 0 of CI/SfB, and the code numbers have been kept the same as in CI/SfB wherever possible to minimise the inconvenience of switching from CI/SfB to Uniclass. However, section 0 of CI/SfB Table 0 (Planning areas) has been modified and moved to section B5 (in the General subjects table). Also some of the sub-sections in section 9 of CI/SfB Table 0 have been moved to other tables. The Utilities, civil engineering facilities section has been heavily revised and expanded.

Concise Table

D1 Utilities, civil engineering facilities

D11 Rail transport facilities
D12 Road transport facilities
D13 Water transport and protection facilities
D14 Air transport facilities
D15 Communications facilities
D16 Power supply, mineral supply facilities
D17 Public health, water engineering facilities

D2 Industrial facilities

D26 Agricultural facilities
D27 Manufacturing facilities by type of industry
D28 Manufacturing facilities by type of premises

D3 Administrative, commercial, protective service facilities

D31 Official administrative facilities, law courts
D32 Office facilities
D33 Commercial facilities
D34 Trading facilities, shops
D37 Protective service facilities

D4 Medical health, welfare facilities

D41 Medical facilities (hospitals)
D42 Primary health care facilities
D44 Welfare facilities, homes
D46 Animal welfare facilities

D5 Recreational facilities

D51 Refreshment and culinary facilities
D52 Entertainment facilities
D53 Social recreation facilities
D54 Swimming facilities
D56 Sports facilities
D58 Amusement, play, tourist facilities
D59 Other recreational facilities

D6 Religious facilities

D61 Religious centre facilities
D62 Cathedrals
D63 Churches, chapels
D64 Mission halls, meeting houses
D65 Non-Christian places of worship
D66 Residential religious facilities
D67 Funerary facilities, shrines, mortuaries
D69 Other religious facilities

D7 Educational, scientific, information facilities

D71 Education facilities (schools)
D72 Further education facilities
D73 Scientific, computing facilities (laboratories)
D74 Assembly, meeting facilities
D75 Exhibition, display facilities
D76 Information/study facilities (libraries)
D79 Other educational etc. facilities

D8 Residential facilities

D81 Domestic residential facilities, housing
D82 Relaxation facilities, living rooms
D83 Sleeping facilities, bedrooms
D85 Communal residential facilities
D86 Historical residential facilities
D87 Temporary, mobile residential facilities
D89 Other residential facilities

D9 Other facilities

D91 Circulation
D92 Reception, waiting facilities
D94 Sanitary, changing facilities
D95 Cleaning, maintenance facilities
D96 Storage facilities
D97 Plant, control facilities

D1 Utilities, civil engineering facilities

D113 *continued*

6 Cable transport
D11361/3
Industrial, non-passenger cable transport
1 Cableways
2 Aerial ropeways/tramways
3 Cable telphers
D11364/6
Passenger cable transport, ski-lifts
4 Cable car transport
5 Chairlifts
6 Tow lifts
7 Automated guided vehicle systems
9 Other
1 Non-suspended monorail systems

D12 Road transport facilities

Combined codes:
D12:E5 Road bridges

D121 Motorways

D122 Other motor roads
1 Primary roads other than motorways
1 Trunk roads
2 Secondary roads, minor roads
3 By-passes, loop roads, ring roads, radial roads
4 Access roads, drives, approach roads, culs-de-sac
5 Single and dual carriageway roads, grade separated roads
1 Single carriageway roads
2 Dual carriageway roads
3 Grade separated roads
9 Other types of motor roads

D11 Rail transport facilities

Includes railway engineering, rail transportation.
Also includes cable transport such as cableways and ski-lifts.

Combined codes:
D11:E5 Rail bridges

D111 Conventional heavy railways
1 Standard main line railways
2 High speed railways
e.g. the French TGV lines.
3 Suburban heavy railways, secondary lines, branch lines
4 Goods railways

D112 Underground railways, light rail transit systems
1 Underground railways
e.g. London Underground, Paris Metro.
2 Light rail transit running on existing British Rail tracks
e.g. the above-ground parts of Tyne and Wear Metro. Usually these will have an overhead electricity supply.
3 Light rail transit running on special tracks
e.g. Docklands Light Railway. Usually these will get electricity from the tracks, typically via a third rail.
4 Light rail transit/trams running largely on-street
e.g. Manchester Metrolink, Sheffield Supertram.

D113 Other railways, cable transport, guided vehicle systems
1 Mountain/steep gradient railways
1 Rack railways
2 Cable railways
3 Funicular railways
4 Adhesion railways
2 Guideway-based rail transport, overhead railways
1 Monorails (overhead)
2 Magnetic levitation transport
3 Telpher lines
3 Light railways
Excludes light rail transit systems.
4 Narrow-gauge railways

D114 Embarkation facilities for rail transport
1 Railway stations, passenger terminals
2 Goods terminals
3 Halts, stops
4 Platforms
5 Station halls
6 Ticket offices
7 Forecourts
9 Other embarkation facilities for rail transport

D115 Permanent way/track
1 Plain line
2 Switches
3 Junctions
4 Sidings
5 Level crossings

D116 Rail vehicle control facilities
1 Signal boxes
2 Signals
4 Marshalling yards
5 Railway relay buildings
6 Railway lineside staff accommodation

D117 Rail vehicle storage/repair facilities
1 Service inspection sheds
2 Repair sheds
3 Bogie drop buildings
4 Wheel lathes
5 Carriage cleaning facilities

D119 Other rail transport facilities

D123 Roads other than motor roads
1 Pedestrian streets
2 Cycle tracks
3 Bridleways
4 Footpaths (field paths, footways, paths), towpaths
8 Other types of road

D124 Embarkation facilities for road transport
1 Coach stations
2 Bus stations
3 Bus stops/shelters

D125 Car parks, parking facilities
1 Underground car parks
2 Surface car parks, street parking
3 Multi-storey car parks
4 Car ramps

D126 Road vehicle service, storage and repair facilities
1 Service stations/petrol stations
1 Petrol stations without major shops/catering facilities
2 Major service stations with major shops/catering facilities
Usually motorway service stations
3 Car washes
2 Spare parts/accessories shops
3 Showrooms
4 Repair/maintenance facilities, repair shops
1 Inspection pits
2 Degreasing/lubricating/ body building units
5 Garages (commercial/large-scale)
"Garages" is used here in the sense: building or space in which motor vehicles are housed.
See D1261 for service stations.
See D1264 for repair/ maintenance facilities.
See D962 for domestic garages.

D127   **Traffic calming constructions, road vehicle control facilities**

D128   **Carriageways, paved parts, etc.**
1 Carriageways
   1 Traffic lanes
   2 Junctions/intersections
2 Other paved parts
   1 Slipways
   2 Lay-bys/drive-ins, passing places
   3 Skid pads
   4 Hardstandings, hard shoulders
   5 Pavements/sidewalks
   6 Refuges/islands
   7 Crossings
   9 Other
3 Crash barriers, central reservations
4 Other non-paved parts
   1 Verges, soft shoulders

D13   **Water transport and protection facilities**

Combined codes:
D13:E5 Aqueducts

D131   **Ship sheltering and berthing facilities, harbours, docks**
See D2755 for Shipbuilding, marine engineering facilities (shipyards).
1 Breakwaters, harbour walls, pierheads
2 Jetties, piers, landing stages
3 Docks
   1 Wet docks
   2 Dry docks
   3 Floating docks
   4 Dock walls
   5 Entrances and locks
   6 Lock gates and caissons
   7 Slipways
   8 Pumping stations for docks
4 Quays, wharves
5 Gangways
7 Rope guiding and fixing devices
   i.e. capstans, fairleads, bollards.
8 Mooring facilities (for light craft)
   Marinas, mooring buoys, etc.

D132   **Port facilities, ports**
Classify here general information on ports and their associated harbours.
1 Cargo storage facilities
   Includes containers, silos, bunkers, transit sheds, etc.
2 Cargo loading/unloading facilities
   Includes cranes, conveyors, etc.
3 Passenger embarkation facilities
   Includes terminals, ramps, walkways and stairs.
4 Boat storage, repair facilities

D132   *continued*
5 Port services facilities
   Includes fire-fighting facilities, tugboats, harbour dredging, navigational facilities.
9 Other port facilities

D133   **Boat control facilities, general**
See also D1327 Port services facilities.
1 Channel dredging
2 Channel demarcation
   1 Marking buoys
   2 Audible marking devices
   3 Radio and radar systems
   4 Lighthouses, light-beacons and light-vessels
   5 Other demarcation systems
3 Coastguard and lifeboat stations

D134   **Canals**
1 Pounds
2 Summit canals
3 Winding holes
4 Canal linings
5 Locks
6 Lock gates
7 Lock chambers
9 Other

D136   **Offshore structures, platforms**
See D1651 for specific information on oil rigs; D1661 for specific information on gas rigs.
1 Fixed offshore structures
   1 Compliant offshore structures
   2 Gravity platforms
2 Mobile offshore structures
   1 Jack-up structures
   2 Semi-submersible structures
3 Drilling platforms
4 Production platforms
   1 Tethered leg platforms
5 Hybrid platforms
6 Offshore modules

D137   **Protective works**
Combined codes:
D137:B5 Coastal planning
D137:E32 Sea walls
1 Wave protection works
   1 Wave screens
   2 Wave walls
   3 Wave deflectors
   4 Spending beaches
2 Erosion protection works
   1 Revetments
   2 Groynes
3 Flood prevention works
   1 Flood banks
   2 Counter walls
   3 Beach bumpings
   4 Floodgates

D14   **Air transport facilities**

D141   **Airports**
An airport is defined as: an air transport facility used by civil aircraft for the carriage of passengers or cargo, or both, and having customs clearance facilities. Use this class number for specific airports; sub-divide alphabetically.
1 International airports, airports for large airliners
2 Airports limited to smaller airliners

D142   **Aerodromes etc.**
1 Landing strips, small aerodromes for light aircraft
2 Heliports
3 VTOL (Vertical take-off and landing) facilities
4 STOL (Short take-off and landing) facilities
5 Military aerodromes
6 Aerodromes for seaplanes

D143   **Airport management and control facilities**
1 Air traffic control towers
3 Lighting systems
4 Aircraft approach guidance systems
5 Navigational systems

D144   **Runway, taxiway and apron facilities**
1 Runways, runway strips
   Includes runways, stopways and surrounding obstruction-free areas.
2 Taxiways
3 Aprons
4 Aircraft stands
7 Other paved areas
8 Other obstruction-free areas over which aircraft can move
   Includes shoulders and cleared zones.

D145   **Airport services facilities**
1 Hangars for repair and storage of aircraft
4 Fuel supply facilities
9 Other airport services facilities

D146   **Embarkation facilities, terminals**
1 Passenger facilities, terminals
   For travellators see L7721.
2 Cargo facilities, terminals
3 Baggage handling facilities
4 Piers and loading bridges linking terminal buildings to aircraft
9 Other parts of embarkation facilities, terminals

D149   **Other air transport facilities**

Facilities

D15 Communications facilities

D151 General broadcasting facilities

D152 Radio facilities

D153 Television facilities
See D5273 for Television studios.
1 Closed circuit television facilities

D154 Telephone, telegraph facilities
1 Telephone facilities
  1 Telephone exchanges
  2 Telephone engineering centres/TSCVs
2 Telegraph facilities
  1 Telex facilities
  2 Facsimile transmission facilities
  3 Data communications facilities

D156 Other telecommunications facilities
1 Fibre optic cable facilities
2 Other cable/line facilities
  See also D154.
3 Microwave beam facilities
4 Laser beam facilities
5 Radio wave facilities
6 Transmission facilities
  i.e. transmitting, receiving and monitoring stations.
  1 Satellite ground stations
7 Switching facilities
  1 Exchanges
  2 Switching centres
  3 Telecommunication control facilities

D157 Postal communications facilities
1 Post offices
2 Sorting offices
4 Parcels offices
5 Mail rooms

D159 Other communications facilities
1 Communication reception/control rooms
  1 Switchboards
2 Telephone booths
3 Telephone boxes

D16 Power supply, mineral supply facilities

D161 Electricity generation
For cooling towers see E64.
1 Coal-fired power stations
2 Oil-fired power stations
3 Dual-fired power stations
4 Nuclear power stations
  1 Magnox stations
  2 Advanced gas cooled stations
  3 Pressurised water reactor stations

D161 *continued*
5 Hydroelectric and pumped storage stations
  1 Pumping systems for pumped storage stations
6 Gas turbine power stations
7 Electricity generation from wave, solar, wind power
  1 Wave power
  2 Solar power
    See also D1644.
  3 Wind power
9 Other electricity generation facilities
  1 Precipitators
  2 Turbine halls
  3 Boiler houses

D162 Combined heat and power generating stations

D163 Electricity transmission and supply facilities
1 Electricity substations
2 Overground transmission facilities
  For pylons see E65.
  For cables, power lines see E72.
3 Underground transmission

D164 Non-electrical power generation and supply
1 Traditional windmills
2 Traditional watermills
3 Direct supply of heat from geothermal sources
4 Direct supply of heat from the sun
  See also D16172.
5 Other direct supply of heat

D165/7
Fossil fuel extraction, supply facilities

D165 Oil (petroleum) extraction, supply facilities
1 Oil rigs, extraction from beneath ocean floor
  See D136 for general information on offshore platforms.
2 Oil wells, extraction from land
3 Oil refineries
4 Oil storage facilities

D166 Gas extraction, supply facilities
D1661/5
Natural gas
1 Gas rigs
  See D136 for general information on offshore platforms.
2 Gas wells
3 Gas treatment facilities
4 Gas storage facilities
  Combined codes:
  D1664:E41 Gasometers/gasholders
5 Gas pipelines
6 Synthetic gas (from coal etc.) production and supply facilities

D167 Solid fuel extraction, supply facilities
1 Coal mines, shaft mines/pits
  Classify general information on coal mines here.
2 Opencast mines
  Includes open cast coal mines.
3 Peat cutting facilities
4 Uranium mines

D168 Mineral extraction, supply facilities
Excludes fossil fuels.
1 Mines for mineral extraction
  See also D1671.
2 Opencast workings for mineral extraction
  See also D1672.
3 Quarries for mineral extraction

D169 Other power supply, mineral supply facilities

D17 Public health, water engineering facilities

Includes solid waste disposal.

D171/4
Public health facilities

D171 Water supply facilities
1 Water supply storage facilities
  For reservoirs see D175.
  Combined codes:
  D1711:E42 Water tanks, water towers
  1 Wells
2 Water supply treatment facilities, water works
  1 Screening plant
  2 Mixing and flocculation plant
  3 Sedimentation plant
  4 Sand filters
  5 Disinfecting plant
  6 Water softening plant
  7 Sludge treatment plant
  8 Other water supply treatment facilities
3 Water supply distribution facilities
  1 Pumping stations
  2 Water mains
  3 Break pressure tank
9 Other water supply facilities

D172 Wet waste facilities
1 Wet waste collection
  1 Small-scale collection, cesspools, septic tanks
  2 Domestic and general collection
    1 Combined sewerage systems
    2 Separate sewerage systems
    3 Partially separate sewerage systems
  3 Industrial collection
  4 Collection from other particular types of facilities
  6 Sewage pumping stations
  9 Other collection facilities
2 Sewage treatment facilities
  1 Package plant and other small scale plant
  2 Preliminary treatment plant, stormwater
  3 Primary settlement plant
  4 Secondary treatment plant
  5 Tertiary treatment plant
  6 Sludge removal and treatment plant
  7 Pumping systems and power units
  8 Control, measuring and transport devices
  9 Other sewage treatment facilities
3 Wet waste disposal facilities
  1 Disposal into sea, outfalls
  2 Disposal into inland waters
  3 Disposal into ground
  4 Disposal onto the land
  5 Incineration of unwanted sludge
9 Other wet waste facilities

D173 Refuse disposal facilities
1 Refuse collection/storage facilities
2 Refuse treatment facilities
  Separators, pulverisers, compactors, etc.
3 Refuse tips/dumps/re-use facilities
4 Incinerators
5 Car barbecue plant
9 Other refuse disposal facilities

D174 Mineral waste disposal facilities
1 Slag heaps
2 Nuclear fission waste products disposal facilities

D175/8
Water engineering facilities
....

D175 Reservoirs
For dams see E33.
1 Natural reservoirs
2 Impounding reservoirs
3 Service reservoirs

D176 Spillways, energy dissipating works
1 Bellmouth spillways
2 Ski jump spillways
3 Siphon spillways
4 Side channel spillways
5 Auxiliary spillway
6 Fuse plug spillways
7 Bye channels
9 Other energy dissipating works

D177 Weirs, barrages
1 Spillweirs
2 Fixed crest weirs
3 Broad-crested weirs
4 Thin-plate weirs
5 Full-width weirs
6 Measuring weirs
  1 Crump weirs
7 Diversion weirs
8 Barrages, barriers

D178 Irrigation/land drainage facilities
Combined codes:
D178:E75 Irrigation/land drainage ditches/channels
1 Checks
....

D179 Other public health facilities

D26 Agricultural facilities

D261 Forestry facilities
1 Shelter belt facilities

D262 Fishing facilities
1 Fisheries
2 Fish farms

D263 Farming facilities
1 Farms
2 Crofts

D264 Horticultural (market gardening) facilities
1 Nurseries
2 Hothouses
3 Glasshouses, greenhouses
4 Agricultural produce facilities

D265 Livestock facilities
Only use this section for agricultural livestock facilities – use D464 for animal welfare facilities according to types of animals.
3 For horses
  1 Studs
4 For cattle
  1 Cattle unit
  2 Cowshed
  3 Milking parlour
5 For sheep, goats
  1 Sheep dipping facilities
6 For pigs
7 For birds, poultry
  1 Battery facilities
  2 Free-range facilities
  3 Barn facilities
9 For other animals

D268 Miscellaneous agricultural facilities
1 Agricultural storage
  Combined codes:
  D2681:E43 Silos, tanks, bins, hoppers
  1 Bulk storage with thrust resistant walls
  2 Storage with non-thrust resistant walls
  3 Storage with little or no wall, Dutch barns
  4 Controlled environment facilities
  5 Manure storage facilities, dungsteads, farm effluent tanks, slurry tanks
2 Fields for containing animals
3 Fields for growing crops
4 Yards
5 Stalls, pens for animals

D27 Manufacturing facilities by type of industry

When required an entry from this section may be coloned with an entry from section D28, for example:
D282:D2761 Factory for textiles production.

D272 Construction industry
1 Builders' yards
2 Local authority maintenance depots

D273 Food, drink, tobacco industries
1 Abattoirs
2 Dairies
3 Breweries
4 Bakeries
5 Canning/bottling
6 Tobacco
9 Other food, drink and tobacco industries

D274 Chemical and allied industries

D275 Engineering industries, metal industries
1 Metals
2 Mechanical engineering
3 Instrument engineering
4 Electrical and electronic engineering
5 Shipbuilding and marine engineering
6 Vehicles
9 Other metal goods

D276 Textile/clothing industries
1 Textiles
2 Leather, leather goods and fur
3 Clothes/footwear

D277 Clay/cement/timber industries
1 Brick manufacturing
2 Pottery manufacturing
3 Glass manufacturing
4 Cement manufacturing
5 Timber manufacturing
6 Furniture manufacturing
7 Paper manufacturing
8 Printing and publishing

D279 Other manufacturing, production facilities by type of industry

D28 Manufacturing facilities by type of premises

When required an entry from this section may be coloned with an entry from section D27, for example:
D282:D2761 Factory for textiles production.

D281 Heavy industry facilities
1 Works
2 Mills

D282 Factories
1 Advance factories/standard factories
2 Flatted factories
3 Industrial workshops
4 Purpose built factories

D283 Light industrial facilities, business parks for light industry
For business parks consisting mainly of office buildings see D32, but classify business parks in general here.

D284 Industrial warehouses, storage facilities
See D96 for storage facilities in general.
1 Advance warehouses/stores
2 Purpose built warehouses/ stores

D285 Industrial process facilities
1 Assembly line facilities
2 Industrial work facilities
3 Production machine rooms

D286 Industrial repair facilities

D287 Distribution centres

D289 Other industrial facilities

D3 Administrative, commercial, protective service facilities

Use this class number for mixed commercial developments of shops, offices, flats, etc.

D31 Official administrative facilities, law courts

D311 International legislative and administrative facilities
1 European parliament
2 UN

D312 National legislative and administrative facilities
1 Parliaments
2 Capitols
3 Ministries

D314 Regional and local legislative and administrative facilities
1 Regional, county and district offices
2 Civic centres
3 County, city and town halls
4 Guildhalls
5 Mayor's parlours
6 Governor's residences

D315 Local offices of government departments
1 Taxation facilities/customs houses
2 Labour exchange facilities
 1 Job centres
 2 Employment exchanges
3 Benefit offices/Department of Social Security offices
4 Local housing offices

D316 Official representation facilities
1 Palaces
2 Presidential residences
3 Embassies
4 Consulates
5 Legations
6 High commissions
7 Missions

D317 Law courts
See D3767 for Cells in general.
Combined codes:
D317:D3767 Cells for Law courts
1 Civil courts
 1 County courts
 2 Magistrates courts
2 Criminal courts/assizes
3 Court rooms

D319 Other official administrative facilities
2 Ceremonial suites
3 Robing rooms
4 Debating chambers

D32   Office facilities

D321   **Business parks consisting of office buildings**
See D283 for business parks in general.

D322   **Purpose built office facilities**

D323   **Office facilities built speculatively**

D324   **Open-plan office facilities, landscaped office facilities, bürolanschaft**

D325   **Traditional office facilities**
i.e. non open-plan offices.

D327   **Art/design studios, drawing offices**
See D527 for film, music and TV studios.
See D734 for photography studios.

D329   **Other office facilities**
1   Typing/word processing pools
2   Executives' offices

D33   Commercial facilities

D334   **High street banks, building societies**
1   With offices/accommodation
2   Without offices/accommodation

D335   **Insurance facilities**
1   Underwriting facilities

D337   **Investment facilities**
1   Stock exchanges
2   Stockbroking facilities
    1   Dealers desks

D339   **Other commercial facilities**
1   Banking halls
2   Safe deposits
3   Tellers boxes

D34   Trading facilities, shops

Use this class number for:
mixed retail developments;
retail/leisure developments where retail facilities form the major part of the development;
out of town retail developments.

D341   **Wholesaling, auction and market facilities, etc.**
1   Wholesaling/factory retail facilities
2   Mail order/catalogue sales facilities
3   Auction facilities
4   Livestock markets
5   Markets (other than livestock)
    1   Open air markets
    2   Indoor markets
6   Multiple trading markets
7   Utilities service centres

D342   **Shopping centres, malls and arcades**
For food courts see D5192.

D343   **Department stores**

D344   **Supermarkets, food superstores**
1   Food superstores
    These have a Net Internal Area (NIA) of greater than 2500 m².
2   Supermarkets
    These have a Net Internal Area (NIA) of less than 2500 m².

D345   **High street shops**

D346   **Corner shops, kiosks**

D347   **Retail facilities by type of goods sold**
1   Food shops
2   Durable goods shops
3   Pharmacies
4   Florists
5   Service shops
6   Craft workshops/shops
7   DIY, hardware shops
9   Other shops

D348   **Dealers, merchants**
1   Coal merchants
2   Builders' merchants
3   Plumbers' merchants

D349   **Other trading facilities**
1   Shops with office, domestic accommodation
2   Shop showrooms
3   Booking halls
4   Fitting rooms
5   Stalls at markets

D37   Protective service facilities

D371   **Rescue/aid facilities**
See D1333 for Coastguard, lifeboat stations.
1   Fire service facilities, stations
    1   Fire training towers
2   Ambulance facilities, stations
3   Mountain rescue facilities
4   Air rescue facilities
5   Air sea rescue facilities

D374   **Police stations, law enforcement facilities**
See D317 for Law courts.
See D3767 for Cells in general.
Combined codes:
D374:D3767   Cells for police stations

D375   **Military facilities**
Classify here military buildings in general.
1   Air force facilities
2   Navy facilities
3   Army facilities, general armed forces facilities
    1   Territorial army centres
4   Civil defence facilities
5   Camps, depots, bases, ranges, missile sites, early warning stations
6   Blockhouses, city walls
7   Air raid shelters, fall out shelters
9   Other military facilities

D376   **Detention, secure facilities, prisons**
See D966 for Secure storage.
1   Open prisons
2   Closed prisons
    1   Semi-secure prisons
    2   Secure prisons
3   Maximum security prisons
4   Remand centres, bail hostels
5   Young offenders institutions, borstals
    Approved schools see D7175.
6   Assessment centres
7   Cells
9   Other detention facilities

D379   **Other protective service facilities**

D4 Medical, health, welfare facilities

Combined codes:
D4:D73 Medical/ pharmaceutical research facilities

D41 Medical facilities (hospitals)

D411 Tertiary, teaching hospitals

D412 District general hospitals

D413 Other types of hospitals, units connected with hospitals
1 Small local hospitals, cottage hospitals
2 Private hospital facilities, hospitals
3 Day hospital facilities, hospitals
4 Field hospitals
5 Psychiatric hospitals, psychiatric units
6 Long stay hospitals, long stay units
7 Maternity, gynaecological units
8 Children's hospitals, paediatric care facilities
9 Other

D414 Core hospital facilities
1 Wards/inpatients facilities
2 Outpatients facilities
3 Accident and emergency, casualty
4 Intensive care
5 Operating theatres, surgery facilities
6 Diagnosis facilities and radiology (X-ray diagnosis, radiotherapy)
7 Rehabilitation/physical medicine (physiotherapy, occupational therapy, speech therapy, etc.)
8 Central supply facilities

D415 Specialised hospital facilities by part of body
1 Ear, nose and throat
2 Dental
  Dentists' surgeries see D424.
3 Heart
4 Eye
5 Feet/chiropody
6 Spinal Injuries, neurological
7 Orthopaedics
9 Other
  1 Genito-urinary
  2 Dermatology
  3 Renal

D416 Other specialised hospital facilities
1 Geriatric care facilities
2 Burns units
3 Limb fitting centres
4 Cancer care facilities, cancer hospitals
5 Care for AIDS patients
6 Isolation units
9 Other

D417 Auxiliary/service hospital facilities
Combined codes:
D417:D32 Hospital administration facilities
D417:D51 Hospital catering facilities
D417:D73 Hospital laboratories, analysis facilities
D417:D767 Medical records facilities
D417:D951 Hospital laundries
1 Pathology, forensic facilities
2 Pharmaceutical manufacture, pharmacy
9 Other

D419 Other hospital facilities, hospitals
1 Consulting rooms for hospitals

D42 Primary health care facilities

D421 Health centres
These are facilities which combine clinics with premises for GP practices, and sometimes have minor surgery and accident and emergency facilities.
1 Health centres with minor surgery and accident and emergency facilities, day surgery health centres
2 Health centres without minor surgery and accident and emergency facilities

D422 Specialised clinics
1 Maternity, ante natal and child clinics
2 Geriatric clinics
3 Screening clinics
4 Addiction treatment clinics
5 Artificial limb centres
9 Other

D423 Premises for GP practices
Where not classified under health centres above.

D424 Dental surgeries

D425 Sick bays

D426 First aid posts

D427 Special centres
1 Blood donation/transfusion centres
2 Health education centres

D428 Parts of primary health care facilities
1 Consulting rooms (non-hospital)

D429 Other primary health care facilities

D44 Welfare facilities, homes

D441 Day centres, welfare consultation centres
1 Crèches, nurseries
2 Counselling centres
3 Citizens advice bureaux
4 Housing advice centres
9 Other

D442 Residential institutions/homes
Homes may be differentiated from housing by the fact that homes have communal dining.
1 Nursing homes
2 Hospices
3 Convalescent homes
4 Sanatoria
9 Other

D446/7
Welfare facilities by type of user

D446 By age of user
1 Children
2 Elderly people

D447 By other characteristics of user
1 Chronic invalids, terminally ill people
2 Mentally ill
3 Mentally handicapped
4 Physically handicapped
5 Addicts
6 Homeless people
7 Victims of abuse
8 People with marriage problems
9 People on probation

D448 Parts of welfare facilities
1 Overnight accommodation
2 Short stay accommodation
3 Long stay accommodation

D46   Animal welfare facilities

D461   Veterinary hospitals

D462   Animal clinics, dispensaries

D463   Animal clipping and pedicuring facilities

D464   Animal rearing and living facilities
For agricultural livestock facilities according to types of animals see D265.
For zoos see D751.
For aviaries for display purposes, as opposed to rearing and living purposes, see D752.
1 Fish
2 Cats, dogs (kennels)
3 Horses (stables)
Combined codes:
D4643:D544   Hippotherapy pools (hydrotherapy pools for horses)
4 Cattle
5 Sheep, goats
6 Pigs
7 Birds, poultry
9 Other animal living and rearing facilities

D465   Quarantine facilities

D469   Other animal welfare facilities

D5   Recreational facilities

Use this class number for leisure/retail developments where leisure facilities form the major part of the development.

D51   Refreshment and culinary facilities

See D12612 for Motorway service station facilities.

D511   Canteens, refectories

D512   Restaurants, cafés, snack bars, coffee bars, tea shops

D513   Fast food restaurants, take-aways

D515   Public houses etc.
1 Public houses
2 Bars
3 Taverns
4 Cocktail lounges
5 Tap rooms
6 Beer gardens
7 Function rooms
9 Other licensed premises

D517   Dining rooms

D518   Food preparation, storage facilities, kitchens
1 Larders
2 Cook/chill facilities
3 Waste food handling facilities

D519   Other refreshment facilities
1 Banqueting rooms
2 Food courts

D52   Entertainment facilities

D521   Entertainment arenas
Venues for large entertainment events.
See also D5612 Sporting arenas.

D522   Dancing, musical facilities
1 Bandstands
2 Dance halls
3 Ballrooms
4 Discotheques/night clubs specialising in popular dance music
5 Rock music venues
8 Dance floors
9 Other musical, dancing facilities

D524   Drama, operatic, concert facilities
1 Theatres
2 Opera houses
3 Concert halls

D525   Leisure boxes, family entertainment venues, cinemas
1 Leisure boxes, family entertainment venues
These combine a cinema with other entertainment facilities and refreshment facilities.
2 Multiplex cinemas
3 Other cinemas

D526   Circuses
1 Circus rings

D527   Entertainment production facilities
1 Film studios
2 Music recording studios
3 Television studios
9 Other entertainment production facilities

D529   Other entertainment facilities
1 Rehearsal, practice facilities
2 Stages, performance facilities
3 Auditoria (audience facilities)
4 Orchestra facilities, pits

D53   Social recreation facilities

D532   Community centres
1 Cultural centres
2 Arts centres
3 Village halls, general purpose community halls

D534   Clubs (non residential, non-commercial)
1 Youth centres
2 Students unions

D536   Residential clubs

D537   Commercial clubs, night clubs
For night clubs specialising in popular dance music see D5224.

D539   Other social recreation facilities

D54 Swimming facilities

Combined codes:
D54:E832 Swimming pools with retractable roofs
D54:F73 Outdoor swimming pools
D54:F75 Indoor swimming pools

D541/4
Swimming facilities by main type of activity

These sections are intended for whole facilities, which may be complexes, buildings or spaces. For classifying particular kinds of pool within a whole facility see D546.

D541 Swimming facilities
i.e. facilities primarily for swimming competition/training.

D542 Leisure pool facilities
i.e. facilities for swimming and water based leisure activities involving slides, pipes, etc.

D543 Diving facilities

D544 Hydrotherapy facilities
Combined codes:
D544:D4643 Hippotherapy pools facilities (hydrotherapy facilities for horses)

D545 Lido facilities
Classify here lidos mainly for swimming etc. For lidos mainly for boating/sailing use D5678.

D546 Pool itself
This section is intended for particular kinds of pool within a whole facility. For classifying whole facilities see D541/4.
1 50 m competition swimming pools
2 Other competition/training swimming pools
3 Diving pools
4 Flexible pools
   i.e. pools whose length and/or depth can be changed
5 Leisure pools
6 Wave pools
7 Whirlpools/spa pools
9 Other types of pool
   1 Water polo pools
   2 Hydrotherapy pools
   3 Splash pools

D547 Slides, flumes, diving boards, wave generation, etc.
1 Slides
2 Flumes/tubes
3 Run outs
4 River rides/tyre rides/tub rides
5 Diving boards
6 Wave generation plant

D549 Other swimming pool and related facilities

D56 Sports facilities

D567 is used to classify sports facilities by type of sport, and class numbers from that section may be used either on their own or coloned with other class numbers in section D56.
For example, Soccer facilities are classified at D56732. If we wanted to be more precise and classify "Stadia for soccer" we could use the class number D561:D56732.
However, where a particular sport is always played in a particular type of facility there is no need to specify the type of facility as well as the sport.
For example squash courts can be simply classified at D56723.

D561 Stadia, arenas, complexes
Only sub-divide this section as below if such distinctions are required.
1 Stadia
   These are venues for large spectator sport events. See also D563.
2 Sports arenas
   These are similar to stadia, but have also been designed for hosting musical concerts etc. For arenas designed primarily for concerts see D521.
3 Sports complexes
   These are sporting developments which contain a number of facilities, e.g. one stadium, one arena and a swimming pool.

D562 Leisure centres, sports hall facilities
Only sub-divide this section as below if such distinctions are required.
1 Sports hall facilities
   These are facilities which contain a single main room – the sports hall – which is usually suitable for a number of different sports, e.g. badminton, basketball, five-a-side football. However, the facility will usually have attached changing rooms, reception area, etc.
2 Leisure centres
   These are multi-room facilities which may include: sports halls, health/fitness centres, squash courts, swimming pools, etc.
   1 Leisure centres with a sports hall, swimming pool and other sports facilities
      For leisure centres where the swimming pool is the major part of the facility see D54.
   2 Leisure centres with a sports hall and other sports facilities
   3 Leisure centres without a sports hall

D563 Sports grounds, small-scale spectator sport facilities, playing fields

D564 Spectator facilities for sports
1 Grandstands, stands
2 Indoor seating
3 Competitor seating/warm-up areas

D565 Practice/training facilities

D567 Sports facilities by type of sport
1 Gymnastics, health/fitness, combat sports
   1 Gymnastics, acrobatics
   2 Health/fitness, general
      1 Body building and weight lifting
      2 Aerobics
      3 Solaria
   3 Combat sports
      1 Boxing
      2 Fencing
      3 Wrestling
      4 Martial arts
      9 Other combat sports
   4 Climbing
2 Racket sports
   1 Tennis
   2 Badminton
   3 Squash
   4 Fives
   5 Table tennis
   9 Other racket sports
3 Team ball games
   1 Cricket
   2 Soccer
      1 Five-a-side soccer
      2 Eleven-a-side soccer
   3 Rugby
   4 Hockey
   5 Basketball
   6 Netball
   7 Volleyball
   9 Other team ball games

D567   *continued*

    4 Athletics, racing sports
      1 Athletics
        1 Track
        2 Field
      2 Horse racing
      3 Dog racing
      4 Cycle racing
      5 Motorcycle racing
      6 Motor car racing
      9 Other racing sports
    5 Winter sports
      1 Dry slope skiing
      2 Machine-made snow skiing
      3 Natural snow skiing
      4 Toboggan runs
      5 Ice rink sports/leisure
      9 Other winter sports
    6 Equestrian, hunting, fishing
      1 Riding schools
      2 Show jumping
      3 Polo
      4 Fishing
      9 Other
    7 Aiming sports
      1 Golf
      2 Bowling (Crown green)
      3 Bowling (Ten pin)
      4 Snooker, billiards, pool
      5 Darts
      6 Archery
      7 Shooting
    8 Boating, water skiing, air
      sports
      For marinas see D1318.
      1 Sailing
      2 Motor boating
      3 Water skiing
      4 Gliding
      5 Aeronautics
      6 Parachuting, hang gliding,
        parapenting
      9 Other kinds of sports

**D568   Facilities/areas for the playing
of the sport itself**
    1 Courses
    2 Pitches
    3 Courts
    4 Tracks
    5 Pavilions
    6 Ranges
    7 Rings
    9 Other

D569   Other sports facilities

**D58   Amusement, play, tourist
facilities**

D581   Gambling facilities
    1 Casinos
    2 Bookmakers

D583   Amusement facilities
    1 Funfairs
    2 Theme parks
    3 Simulation amusement
      facilities
      *These are amusement facilities
      featuring computer controlled
      and/or computer generated
      simulations.*
      1 Amusement facilities with
        computer controlled special
        effects
      2 Virtual reality amusement
        facilities
    4 Fairgrounds
    5 Show grounds
    6 Amusement arcades

D584   Tourist facilities
    1 Visitor centres
    2 Tourist information centres
    3 Interpretation facilities
      e.g. Jorvik Viking Centre.
    4 Holiday camps
    5 Caravan and camping sites
      Combined codes:
      D5845:D94 Caravan and
      camping site utility blocks

D585   Play facilities
    1 Playgrounds
    2 Adventure playgrounds
    3 Play centres
    4 Play areas/rooms
    5 Large, fixed playground
      equipment
    6 Play accessories

**D586   Field study centres, outdoor
activity centres**

D587   Parks, gardens
    1 Public parks

**D589   Other amusement, play, tourist
facilities**

D59   Other recreational facilities

D61   Religious centre facilities

D611   Episcopal palaces

D612   Deaneries

D613   Pastoral centres

D614   Ecumenical centres

D62   Cathedrals

D621   Chapter houses

D622   Cathedral treasuries
*For other parts of cathedrals see
D631/9.*

D63   Churches, chapels

D631   Chancels
    1 Sanctuaries
    2 Choirs
    3 Altars

D632   Naves, transepts

D633   Crypts

D634   Galleries

**D635   Side chapels, baptisteries,
confessing facilities, preaching
facilities, sacramental facilities**

D636   Ambulatory facilities
For cloisters see F338.
    1 Aisles
    2 Retrochoirs

**D637   Spires, towers, belfries,
campanili**

D638   Vestries

**D639   Other parts of Christian worship
facilities, churches**

Facilities

D64 Mission halls, meeting houses

D65 Non-Christian places of worship

D651 Temples

D652 Mosques

D653 Synagogues

D654 Non-Christian religious meeting places

D659 Parts of non-Christian worship facilities

D66 Residential religious facilities

D661 Convents

D662 Abbeys, monasteries, nunneries, priories, friaries

D663 Retreat centres

D67 Funerary facilities, shrines, mortuaries

D671 Mortuaries, morgues

D672 Crematoria

D673 Cemeteries (graveyards)

D674 Tombs, mausoleums, funeral vaults, shrines, reliquaries

D676 Gardens of remembrance, remembrance pavilions

D677 Funeral parlours, chapels of rest

D679 Other funerary facilities

D69 Other religious facilities

D7 Educational, scientific, information facilities

D71 Education facilities (schools)

D711 Nursery schools

D712 Primary schools
1 Infant schools
2 First schools
3 Junior schools
4 Middle schools
5 Independent primary schools, preparatory schools

D713 Secondary schools
1 Comprehensive schools
  1 Grant maintained
  2 Local authority controlled
2 Grammar schools
3 Independent/private/public schools
  1 Boarding schools
  2 Day schools
  3 Mixed boarding/day schools
5 Technology schools
  i.e. schools with a technological bias, such as city technology schools.
9 Other types of secondary schools

D714 Sixth form colleges, tertiary colleges

D717 Schools for special needs groups
1 Schools for children with learning difficulties, mental handicaps, autism, emotional problems
2 Schools for children with physical handicaps
3 Approved schools
9 Other special needs schools

D718 Parts of education facilities
1 General purpose classrooms
2 Classrooms for science, technology, etc.
  1 Science laboratories
  2 Computer laboratories
  3 Classrooms for woodwork, metalwork, etc.
3 Music rooms
4 Language laboratories
5 Art/design/craft classrooms
6 Sixth form centres/common rooms
9 Other parts of education facilities

D719 Other education facilities

D72 Further education facilities

D721 Universities
1 Traditional universities
2 Former polytechnics

D722 Polytechnics, technical colleges, general colleges of further education

D723 Colleges of education

D724 Colleges of art and design

D725 Colleges/academies of music, drama, dance

D726 Adult education facilities

D727 Learned societies

D728 Parts of further education facilities
1 General purpose lecture theatres
2 General purpose teaching rooms other than lecture theatres
3 General purpose research rooms
4 Science laboratories
  1 For teaching
  2 For research
5 Language laboratories
6 Computer laboratories
9 Other parts of further education facilities

D729 Other further education facilities

D73 Scientific, computing facilities (laboratories)

Combined codes:
D73:D4 Medical/pharmaceutical research facilities
D73:D417 Hospital laboratories, analysis facilities

D731 Computing facilities, computer rooms

D732 Clean rooms

D733 Instrument rooms

D736 Photography facilities
1 Dark rooms

D737 Observatories, recording stations
1 Meteorological stations
2 Geophysical stations
3 Seismographic stations

D739 Other scientific facilities

D74   Assembly, meeting facilities

D741   Conference centres

D742   Trade centres

D75   Exhibition, display facilities

D751   Botanical gardens, herbaria, zoos
For facilities for the purpose of animal rearing and living, as opposed to the purpose of displaying, see D464.

D752   Aviaries
For facilities for the purpose of bird rearing and living, as opposed to the purpose of displaying, see D4647.

D753   Aquaria, oceanaria

D754   Museums, planetariums

D755   Art galleries, facilities for the display of art

D756   Centres for general exhibitions

D757   Centres for special kinds of exhibitions
1 Design centres
2 Building centres
3 Architecture centres

D759   Other exhibition/display facilities

D76   Information/study facilities (libraries)

D761   National libraries

D762   Public libraries

D763   University, college, school libraries

D764   Information facilities by special subject
Classify according to alphabetical order of subjects.

D765   Information facilities by form of material
1 Map libraries
2 Audio-visual libraries
3 Resource centres
4 Drawings/illustrations/ photograph libraries
5 Newspaper libraries

D766   Company libraries, special libraries

D767   Record offices, archives, patent offices

D768   Commercial lending libraries, subscription libraries

D769   Parts of information facilities
1 Lending section
2 Reference section
3 Enquiry area
4 Catalogue area
5 Study areas
6 Photocopying, computing areas
9 Other parts of information facilities

D79   Other educational etc. facilities

D8   Residential facilities

Use this class number for community developments consisting of housing plus other associated facilities.

D81   Domestic residential facilities, housing

D811   Housing by type
Combined codes:
D811:E811   Bungalows
D811:E821   Detached housing
D811:E822   Semi-detached housing
D811:E824   Terraced housing
1 Flats (apartments)
2 Maisonettes

D813   Housing by size of development
1 Individually-designed houses, housing units
2 Small groups of houses, single streets of houses
3 Blocks of flats/maisonettes
4 Housing estates

D814   Housing by occupier
For welfare homes see D442.
1 Old people's housing, sheltered housing
2 Disabled people's housing
3 Housing for mentally ill people
4 Caretakers', wardens' housing
5 Vicarages, rectories, etc.

D815   Housing by owner
1 Owner-occupied housing
2 Owned by private landlord
3 Council housing
4 Housing association housing
5 Speculative housing, housing for unspecified owner

D819   Other domestic residential facilities

D82   Relaxation facilities, living rooms

D83   Sleeping facilities, bedrooms

Facilities

D85 Communal residential facilities

D852 Hotels

D853 Motels

D854 Guesthouses

D855 Hostels
1 Youth hostels
2 Short stay housing

D856 Halls of residence
i.e. flats with communal facilities.

D857 Foyer buildings
i.e. a combination of housing and training facilities for young people, based on the French model.

D858 Parts of communal residential facilities
1 Single hotel bedrooms
   1 With en-suite facilities
   2 Without en-suite facilities
2 Double hotel bedrooms
   1 With en-suite facilities
   2 Without en-suite facilities
3 Suite of hotel rooms
4 Dormitories, communal sleeping areas

D859 Other communal residential facilities

D86 Historical residential facilities

D861 Castles

D862 Chateaux

D863 Fortified houses

D864 Other historical houses

D868 Parts of historical residential facilities

D87 Temporary, mobile residential facilities

D89 Other residential facilities

D9 Other facilities

D91 Circulation

This is only intended for classifying the user activity "circulation", or whole structures devoted to circulation (e.g. link buildings). For circulation spaces see F3.

D92 Reception, waiting facilities

D94 Sanitary, changing facilities

D941 Lavatories, public conveniences

D942 Bathrooms, washing facilities

D943 Saunas, Turkish baths, etc.

D945 Changing, dressing facilities

D95 Cleaning, maintenance facilities

D951 Laundries

D96 Storage facilities

For industrial warehouses see D284.

D961 General purpose storage facilities, cloakrooms, luggage rooms, stock rooms, waste storage facilities

D962 Domestic garages, sheds, etc.
Includes garden sheds, cycle sheds.
For large-scale/commercial garages see D1265.

D963 Liquid storage

D964 Hot storage

D965 Cold storage
1 Refrigerated storage
2 Deep freeze storage

D966 Secure storage

D97 Plant, control facilities

D971 Plant rooms

D972 Control rooms

D973 Services facilities

Construction entities

Definition

A construction entity is an independent construction of significant scale (see Notes overleaf).

This table classifies construction entities according to their physical form/basic function, i.e. construction entities with a similar physical form/basic function are grouped together.

Examples

At the highest level, construction entities fall into two groups: Buildings, and Civil engineering works.

Examples of construction entities which fall into the Civil engineering group are: bridges, roads, dams, towers, retaining walls, pipelines, etc.

Use

This table may be used to classify construction entities according to their physical form or basic function without regard to the type of facility which the construction entity may form a part of. For example, classify at E32 information about the design of retaining walls which may be equally relevant to a highway project, building project or maritime construction project. This table may also be used in combination with the Facilities table if it is necessary to classify both the physical form/basic function and the user activity of a construction entity, for example D11:E5 Rail bridges.

For the classification of construction works according to user activity see Table D.

For Elements of Buildings see Table G.

For Elements of Civil engineering works see Table H.

continued

For those interested in terminology, compare this definition of construction entity with the following terms from ISO 6707/1:

Construction works
Everything that is constructed or results from construction operations.

Civil Engineering Works
Construction works that comprises a structure, such as a dam, bridge, road or the results of operations such as dredging, de-watering, soil stabilisation, but excluding a building and its associated site works.

Building
Construction works that has the provision of shelter for its occupants or contents as one of its main purposes and is normally designed to stand in one place.

The new term, Construction Entities was selected because a term is needed which includes both Buildings and Civil Engineering Works, but which is narrower than all construction works.

Concise Table

E0	**Construction complexes**	**E7**	**Pipelines, ducts, cables and channels**

E1 Pavements and landscaping

E11 Pavements, permanent ways
E12 Hard landscaping
E13 Soft landscaping

E2 Tunnels, shafts, cuttings

E21 Tunnels
E22 Shafts
E23 Cuttings

E3 Embankments, retaining walls, etc.

E31 Embankments
E32 Retaining/protecting walls
E33 Dams

E4 Tanks, silos, etc.

E41 Containers for gases
E42 Tanks for liquids
E43 Silos

E5 Bridges, viaducts

E51 Bridges by material of construction
E52 Simple span bridges
E53 Cantilever bridges
E54 Cable stayed bridges
E55 Suspension bridges
E56 Arch bridges
E57 Movable bridges
E58 Bridges by what carried
E59 Bridges by geometry/scale, other types of bridges

E6 Towers, superstructures (excluding buildings)

E61 Towers
E62 Gantries
E63 Chimneys (free standing)
E64 Cooling towers
E65 Lattice towers, pylons
E66 Masts

E7 Pipelines, ducts, cables and channels

E71 Pipelines
E72 Cables, power lines
E73 Ducts
E74 Manholes, chambers
E75 Channels, trenches, ditches, etc.

E8 Buildings

E81 Buildings defined by height/number of storeys
1 Single storey buildings
2 Two storey buildings
etc....
9 Tall buildings, skyscrapers
E82 Buildings defined by relationship with adjacent buildings
1 Detached buildings
2 Semi-detached buildings
3 Linked/lean-to buildings
4 Terraces/parades
5 Infill buildings
6 Buildings constructed over something, air rights buildings
E83 Buildings defined by special form of construction
1 Buildings with cable tensioned fabric roofs
2 Buildings with retractable roofs
3 Long-span, large volume buildings, supersheds
4 System-built buildings, volumetric buildings
E84 Intelligent buildings
E85 Mobile, demountable, temporary, floating buildings
E86 Underground buildings
E89 Other types of buildings

Codes from this table may be combined with class numbers from Table N Properties and characteristics, e.g.:
E:N246 Earthquake resistant structures
E5:N246 Earthquake resistant bridges

For definitions of terms used in this section see the BSI Glossary of building and civil and engineering terms.

E0   Construction complexes

Two or more adjacent construction entities collectively serving one or more user activity/purpose.

E1   Pavements and landscaping

E11   Pavements, permanent ways
Includes the structure of roads, runways, railways, etc.
1 Rigid pavements
2 Rigid composite pavements
3 Flexible pavements
4 Flexible composite pavements

E12   Hard landscaping

E13   Soft landscaping

E2   Tunnels, shafts, cuttings

E21   Tunnels
1 Adits
2 Pilot tunnels
3 Immersed tube tunnels
4 Headings

E22   Shafts

E23   Cuttings

E3   Embankments, retaining walls, etc.

E31   Embankments

E32   Retaining/protecting walls
Combined codes:
E32:D137   Sea walls
1 Retaining walls
2 Protecting walls

E33   Dams
See also D175   Reservoirs.
1 Embankment dams
  1 Earth dams
  2 Rock fill dams
  3 Hydraulic fill dams
2 Gravity dams
  1 Gabion dams
  2 Crib dams
3 Gravity arch dams
4 Arch dams
5 Buttress dams
  1 Arch buttress dams
  2 Flat slab buttress dams
  3 Solid head buttress dams

E4   Tanks, silos, etc.

E41   Containers for gases
Combined codes:
E41:D1664   Gasometers/gasholders

E42   Tanks for liquids
Combined codes:
E42:D1711   Water tanks, water towers

E43   Silos
Combined codes:
E43:D2681   Silos for agricultural storage

E5   Bridges, viaducts

E51   Bridges by material of construction
These codes may be used as qualifiers for any of the codes in sections E52 to E59.
1 Steel girder bridges
  1 Steel simple beam bridges
  2 Steel lattice girder bridges
  3 Steel truss bridges
  4 Steel box girder bridges
2 Concrete girder bridges
  1 Post-tensioned concrete girder bridges
  2 Pre-tensioned concrete girder bridges
  3 Concrete girder bridges with no pre-stressing
3 Wooden bridges
4 Masonry bridges
8 Composite bridges
9 Other

E52/6
Bridges by structural means of support

E52   Simple span bridges

E53   Cantilever bridges

E54   Cable stayed bridges
These are bridges in which the main structural members are beams supported by one or more straight inclined cables supported by a tower (compare with suspension bridges).

E55   Suspension bridges
These are bridges in which the main suspension elements are cables from which the deck is suspended (compare with cable stayed bridges).

E56   Arch bridges
1 Masonry arch bridges
2 Concrete arch bridges
3 Steel arch bridges

E57   Movable bridges
1 Drawbridges
2 Bascules
3 Vertical lift bridges
4 Swing bridges
5 Retractable bridges
6 Floating bridges
7 Transporter bridges

E58   Bridges by what carried
See D11:E5 for Rail bridges, D12:E5 for Road bridges, D13:E5 for Aqueducts.
1 Foot bridges
2 Bridges carrying buildings
3 Bridges carrying pipes or cables

E59 Bridges by geometry/scale, other types of bridges
1 Skew bridges
2 Curved bridges
3 Large span bridges
4 Multi-span bridges
5 Through-girder bridges
9 Other types of bridges

E6 Towers, superstructures

Excludes buildings.
For stands, grandstands see D56 Sports facilities.
For structures for particular user activities see Table D Facilities.

E61 Towers

E62 Gantries

E63 Chimneys (free standing)

E64 Cooling towers

E65 Lattice towers, pylons
For pylons as an element of cable carrying constructions see H724.

E66 Masts

E7 Pipelines, ducts, cables and channels

E71 Pipelines
Classify general information on pipelines here.
For specific information on pipes carrying cables see E72.
Combined codes:
E71:E75 Trenches for pipelines

E72 Cables, power lines
Includes information on pipes carrying cables.

E73 Ducts
1 Duct networks
2 Jointing chambers
3 Cable tunnels
4 Cable ways

E74 Manholes, chambers

E75 Channels, trenches, ditches, etc.
Classify general information on channels, trenches, ditches here.
For canals see D134.
For specific information on irrigation/land drainage channels/ditches see D178:E75.

E8 Buildings

See F7 for building spaces by degree and type of enclosure, including roofed, open air.
See Table D Facilities for buildings defined according user activity, e.g. hospitals, office buildings, etc.
See Table L Construction products for Pre-fabricated buildings.

E81 Buildings defined by height/ number of storeys
1 Single storey buildings
2 Two storey buildings
3 Three storey buildings
etc. . . .
9 Tall buildings, skyscrapers

E82 Buildings defined by relationship with adjacent buildings
1 Detached buildings
2 Semi-detached buildings
3 Linked/lean-to buildings
4 Terraces/parades
5 Infill buildings
6 Buildings constructed over something, air rights buildings

E83 Buildings defined by special form of construction
1 Buildings with cable tensioned fabric roofs
2 Buildings with retractable roofs
3 Long-span, large volume buildings, supersheds
4 System-built buildings, volumetric buildings

E84 Intelligent buildings

E85 Mobile, demountable, temporary, floating buildings
1 Mobile buildings
2 Demountable buildings
3 Temporary buildings
4 Floating buildings

E86 Underground buildings

E89 Other types of buildings

Spaces

Definition   A space is an area or volume contained within, or otherwise associated with, a building or other construction entity. A space may be bounded physically or notionally.

Examples   Rooms, atria, corridors, courtyards, public space/private space.

Use   Information on the design, regulations/requirements, costs or character of spaces.

Notes   In this table only **building spaces** are classified, since the concept of space is not generally used in connection with other construction entities. By building space we mean any space associated with a building (including balconies, verandahs and space around the building required by fire regulations, etc.). Building spaces may be classified according to:
- Their actual or planned **user activity**. This is achieved by combination with the relevant terms from the Facilities table. For example F:D32 Office space.
- Their **complexity/scale** into one of the following classes: **zones, rooms/circulation spaces, or sub-spaces** (see F1/F4).
- Their **location** in the building, for example which floor they are on (see F13).
- Whether they are **internal** or **external** (see F5/F6).
- The **degree of enclosure** (see F7).
- **Surveying standards** – two possible options are presented here, one based on the RICS and ISVA Code of measuring practice, the other based on ISO 9836:1992 (see F9).
- **Other considerations** such as whether a space is to be a fire compartment, whether it is to be accessible to the public, etc. (see F8).

Concise Table

F1/F4
Building spaces according to complexity/scale

F1   Compound spaces of buildings, zones

F11   Semi-independent parts of a building, blocks
F12   Vertically divided parts of buildings
i.e. wings, bays, core
F13   Horizontally divided parts of buildings, storeys
F19   Other compound spaces, zones
Including user functional departments.

F2   Rooms
Examples of combination with the Facilities table:
D76:F2   Library room
D32:F2   Office room

F3   Circulation spaces
Classify here circulation sub-spaces, such as gangways. Classify here external circulation spaces, such as covered ways, passages.

F4   Building sub-spaces
See F3 for circulation sub-spaces.

F5/F6
Building spaces according to whether they are internal or external

F5   Internal spaces of buildings

F6   External spaces of buildings
See F3 for external circulation spaces.

F7   Building spaces by degree and type of enclosure

F71   Free space
F72   Open space
F73   Not covered, enclosed space
F74   Covered, not enclosed space
F75   Fully enclosed space

F8   Miscellaneous spaces, other spaces

F81   Fire compartments
F82   Protected space
F83   Private space
F84   Public space
F85   Danger area
F89   Other spaces

F9   Building space analysed

F91   Building space analysed according to ISO 9836:1992
1   Usable area
F92   Building space analysed according to RICS and ISVA Code of measuring practice
1   Net Internal Area

Spaces

F

*Spaces are classified according to
user activity by using the colon
sign and codes from Table D
Facilities, for example:*
F:D32 Office space
F:D34 Trading space
F:D41 Medical space
F:D44 Welfare space
F:D56 Sports space
F:D6   Religious space
F:D76 Information/study space

F1/F4
**Building spaces according to
complexity/scale**

| F1 | **Compound spaces of buildings, zones** |

*Zone: a compound space of a
building consisting of a number of
rooms or circulation spaces or
external spaces.*

**F11 Semi-independent parts of a
building, blocks**

**F12 Vertically divided parts of
buildings**
1 Wings
2 Bays
3 Core

**F13 Horizontally divided parts of
buildings, storeys**
1 Sub-basement
2 Basement
3 Semi-basement
4 Ground floor
5 Mezzanine floor
6 First floor and above, but
below highest floor
  01 First floor
  02 Second floor
  03 Third floor
  etc. . . .
  10 Tenth floor
  11 Eleventh floor
  etc. . . .
  99 Ninety-ninth floor
7 Highest floor
8 Space beneath a sloping roof,
attic
9 Space on top of a flat roof
For storage of plant etc.

F19 Other compound spaces, zones
1 User functional departments
*For example: Administration,
Production, etc.
Classify types of department
with reference to the facilities
table, e.g.:
F191:D32 Administration
Department.*

| F2 | **Rooms** |

*Room: a space within a storey,
enclosed by a floor, a ceiling and
walls or fixed partitions, other than
a circulation space.*

*Examples of combination with the
facilities table:*
F2:D76 Study room
F2:D32 Office room

| F3 | **Circulation spaces** |

*Circulation space: a space for the
movement of persons, goods or
vehicles.
Classify here circulation sub-
spaces, such as gangways.
Classify here external circulation
spaces, such as covered ways,
passages.*

11 Porches
14 Entrance halls, foyers
17 Atria
21 Central halls, lobbies
24 Stairs, lift shafts, escalators
27 Corridors
31 Internal balconies, galleries
32 External balconies
  *These may be either
projecting or recessed from
the external face of the
building.*
34 Gangways
37 Covered ways
38 Cloisters
41 Passages, alleys
44 Crawlways
51 Air locks
99 Other circulation spaces

| F4 | **Building sub-spaces** |

See F3 for circulation sub-spaces.

F41 Activity space
*Space required for an activity that
comprises a working space
together with an occupied space.*

F42 Working space
*Space required for installation,
use, operation or maintenance of
an item. For example: space in
front of a wash basin, space to
accommodate a door swing.*

F43 Occupied space
*Space occupied by any equipment
needed to perform an activity.*

F44 Alcoves, niches

F45 Incidental space, voids

F5/F6
**Building spaces according to
whether they are internal or
external**

| F5 | **Internal spaces of buildings** |

*Spaces which lie within the main
building envelope.*

| F6 | **External spaces of buildings** |

*Spaces which lie outside the main
building envelope. These may,
however, be roofed.
See F3 for External circulation
spaces.*

F61 Courtyards, forecourts

F62 Basement areas

F63 Dry areas

F64 Light wells

F65 Terraces
1 Verandahs

F

Spaces

F7	Building spaces by degree and type of enclosure

F71 Free space
i.e. a space with no physical boundaries, only notional ones.

F72 Open space
i.e. a space with a floor, pavement or ground surface, but not covered, and with no or limited horizontal physical boundaries.

F73 Not covered, enclosed space
i.e. a space which is not covered, but is physically bounded horizontally.
1 Partly covered

F74 Covered, not enclosed space
i.e. a space which is covered, but has no or limited horizontal physical boundaries.

F75 Fully enclosed space
i.e. a space which is fully physically bounded on all sides.

F8	Miscellaneous spaces, other spaces

F81 Fire compartments

F82 Protected space

F83 Private space

F84 Public space

F85 Danger area

F89 Other spaces

F9	Building space analysed

Building space analysed according to surveyors' measurement standards.

F91 Building space analysed according to ISO 9836:1992
1 Usable area
The usable area is that part of the total area which corresponds to the purpose and use of the building.
This is similar to, but not exactly the same as, the RICS and ISVA's Net Internal Area.
Examples of combination with the facilities table:
F911:D73 Area usable for science activities
F911:D32 Area usable for office activities
2 Circulation area
3 Services area
e.g. ducts, plant rooms.
4 Structural element area
Includes voids contained within elements.
9 Gross area
Gross area = structural element area
+ usable area
+ circulation area
+ services area.

F92 Building space analysed according to RICS and ISVA Code of measuring practice
1 Net Internal Area
The Net Internal Area is the usable area within a building measured to the internal face of the perimeter walls at each floor level.
This is similar to, but not exactly the same as, the ISO 9836:1992's usable area.
Examples of combination with the facilities table:
F921:D73 Net Internal Area for science activities
F921:D32 Net Internal Area for office activities

Elements for buildings

G

Definition

Element: a major physical part or system of a building or other construction entity, which, in itself or in combination with other elements, fulfils a characteristic predominating function of the building or other construction entity. (Examples of characteristic predominating functions for buildings are: enclosing, furnishing or servicing spaces.) Elements are considered without regard to the type of technical solution or the method or form of construction.

Examples

Floors, roofs, walls, water supply services, lighting services.

Use

Classifying design data, cost analyses and drawings of **buildings**.

For elements of construction entities other than buildings see Table H.

This table is not intended to be used for the classification of product information (see Table L).

Concise Table

G1	**Site preparation**		**G5**	**Services: complete elements**
G11	Site clearance		G50	Water supply
G12	Ground contouring		G51	Gas supply
G13	Stabilisation		G52	Heating/ventilation/ air conditioning (HVAC)
			G53	Electric power
			G54	Lighting
G2	**Fabric: complete elements**		G55	Communications
			G56	Transport
G21	:G311 Foundations *(foundations consist entirely of core fabric)*		G57	Protection
			G58	Removal/disposal
			G59	Other services elements
	G22 Floors			
G221	Lowest floors		**G6**	**Services: parts of elements**
G222	Upper floors			
			G61	Energy generation/storage/ conversion
G23	Stairs		G62	Non-energy treatment/storage
G24	Roofs		G63	Distribution
			G64	Terminals
	G25 Walls		G65	Package units
G251	External walls		G66	Monitoring and control
G252	Internal walls and partitions		G69	Other parts of services elements
G26	Frame/isolated structural members			

G3	**Fabric: parts of elements**		**G7**	**External/site works**
	G31 Carcass/structure/fabric		G71	Surface treatment
G311	Core fabric		G72	Enclosure/division
G312	Coverings/external finishes		G73	Special purpose works
			G74	Fittings/furniture/equipment
	G32 Openings		G75	Mains supply
G321	Windows		G76	External distributed services
G322	Doors		G77	Site/underground drainage
	G33 Internal finishes			
G331	Floor finishes			
G332	Ceilings/soffit finishes			
G333	Wall internal finishes			
G334	Other internal finishes			
G34	Other parts of fabric elements			

G4	**Fittings/furniture/equipment (FFE)**
G41	Circulation FFE
G42	Rest, work FFE
G43	Culinary FFE
G44	Sanitary, hygiene FFE
G45	Cleaning, maintenance FFE
G46	Storage, screening FFE
G47	Works of art, soft furnishings
G48	Special activity FFE *Subdivide by Facilities table.*
G49	Other FFE

Elements for buildings

In this table the combined codes under each main element have been abbreviated for the sake of clarity of presentation. For example, at G24 Roofs, the entry ":G312 Roof coverings" is an abbreviation for "G24:G312 Roof coverings".
The full codes should be used when quoting Uniclass codes.

G1 Site preparation

G11 Site clearance

G12 Ground contouring

G13 Stabilisation

G2 Fabric: complete elements

G21 :G311 Foundations
(foundations consist entirely of core fabric)

G22 Floors

G221 Lowest floors
:G311 Core fabric
:G331 Floor finish to lowest floors
1 Direct
2 Raised floor

G222 Upper floors
:G311 Core fabric
:G331 Floor finish to upper floors
1 Direct
2 Raised floor
:G332 Ceilings/soffit finishes to upper floors
1 Direct
2 Suspended

G23 Stairs
Balustrades are at G251 and G252. However, if preferred, balustrades to stairs/ramps may be included here.
:G311 Core fabric
:G33 Stair finish
11 Top
21 Soffit

G24 Roofs
:G311 Core fabric
:G312 Roof coverings
:G321 Roof lights
:G332 Roof soffit finishes/ ceilings to roofs
1 Direct
2 Suspended
:G34 Roof edges
Includes parapets, gutters, etc. Rainwater downpipes are at G5812.

G25 Walls

G251 External walls
Includes external balustrades.
:G311 Core fabric
:G312 Coverings/external finishes to external walls
:G321 External windows
:G322 External doors
:G333 Internal finish to external walls

G252 Internal walls and partitions
Includes internal balustrades.
:G311 Core fabric
:G321 Internal windows
:G322 Internal doors
:G333 Internal finish to internal walls

G26 Frame/isolated structural members
:G311 Core fabric
:G334 Frame finish
Where separate from ceiling and wall finishes.

G3 Fabric: parts of elements

G31 Carcass/structure/fabric

G311 Core fabric
:G21 Foundations
(foundations consist entirely of core fabric)
:G221 Core fabric of lowest floors
:G222 Core fabric of upper floors
:G23 Core fabric of stairs
:G24 Core fabric of roofs
:G251 Core fabric of external walls
:G252 Core fabric of internal walls
:G26 Core fabric of frame

G312 Coverings/external finishes
:G24 Coverings of roofs
:G251 Coverings/external finishes to external walls

G32 Openings

G321 Windows
:G24 Roof lights
:G251 External windows
:G252 Internal windows

G322 Doors
:G251 External doors
:G252 Internal doors

G33 Internal finishes

G331 Floor finishes
1 Floor finishes, direct
:G221 To lowest floors
:G222 To upper floors
:G23 To stairs
2 Floor finishes, raised
:G221 To lowest floors
:G222 To upper floors

G332 Ceilings/soffit finishes
1 Ceilings/soffit finishes, direct
:G222 To upper floors
:G23 To stairs
:G24 To roofs
2 Ceilings/soffit finishes, suspended
:G222 To upper floors
:G24 To roofs

G333 Wall internal finishes
:G251 To external walls
:G252 To internal walls

G334 Other internal finishes
:G26 Frame finishes
Where separate from ceiling and wall finishes.

G34 Other parts of fabric elements
:G24 Roof edges
Includes parapets, gutters, etc. Rainwater downpipes are at G5812.

G4 Fittings/furniture/equipment (FFE)

G41 Circulation FFE

G42 Rest, work FFE

G43 Culinary FFE

G44 Sanitary, hygiene FFE

G45 Cleaning, maintenance FFE

G46 Storage, screening FFE

G47 Works of art, soft furnishings
1 Works of art
2 Soft furnishings

G48 **Special activity FFE**
Classify with reference to
Table D Facilities.

G49 **Other FFE**

G5 **Services: complete elements**

G50 **Water supply**
For mains water supply see G751.
Classify parts with reference to
Section G6, e.g.:
G50:G61 Energy generation/
storage/conversion for water
supply
G50:G632 Pipework for water
supply
G502:G632 Pipework for hot
water supply
1 Cold water
2 Hot water
9 For special activity
Classify with reference to
Table D Facilities.

G51 **Gas supply**
For mains gas supply see G754.
Classify parts with reference to
Section G6, e.g.:
G51:G632 Pipework for gas
supply

G52 **Heating/ventilation/air**
conditioning (HVAC)
Classify parts with reference to
Section G6, e.g.:
G52:G61 Energy generation/
storage/conversion for HVAC
G52:G631 Ductwork for HVAC
1 Heating
2 Heating + non-cooling air
conditioning
3 Heating + cooling air
conditioning
4 Ventilation
1 Supply and extract ventilation
2 Extract ventilation
For smoke extraction/control
see G5723.
9 For special activity
Classify with reference to
Table D Facilities, e.g.:
G529:D73 Special HVAC
services for laboratories

G53 **Electric power**
For electric mains see G755.
Classify parts with reference to
Section G6, e.g.:
G53:G61 Energy generation/
storage/conversion for electric
power
1 General purpose outlets
2 Supply to services
installations
9 For special activity
Classify with reference to
Table D Facilities.

G54 **Lighting**
For outdoor lighting see G761.
Classify parts with reference to
Section G6.
1 General lighting
2 Emergency lighting
9 For special activity
Classify with reference to
Table D Facilities.

G55 **Communications**
Classify parts with reference to
Section G6.
1 Public address
2 Visual display
3 Radio
4 TV
5 Telephones
6 Computer networks
9 For special activity
Classify with reference to
Table D Facilities, e.g.:
G559:D14 Special
communications services for air
transport

G56 **Transport**
Classify parts with reference to
Section G6.
1 Lifts/hoists
2 Escalators
3 Conveyors
4 Travelling cradles
9 For special activity
Classify with reference to
Table D Facilities, e.g.:
G569:D284 Special transport
services for industrial
warehouses (including
mechanical handling systems)

G57 **Protection**
Classify parts with reference to
Section G6.
1 Security
1 Entrance controls
2 Intruder/security alarms
2 Fire
1 Fire/smoke alarms
2 Fire fighting and sprinkler
installations
3 Smoke extraction/control
installations
3 Other protection
1 Lightning protection
9 For special activity
Classify with reference to
Table D Facilities.

G58 **Removal/disposal**
Classify parts with reference to
Section G6.
1 Drainage
1 Foul drainage
2 Surface water drainage
Includes rainwater
downpipes. Gutters are at
G24:G34.
2 Refuse disposal
9 For special activity
Classify with reference to
Table D Facilities.

G59 **Other services elements**

G6 **Services: parts of elements**

For mains supply see G75.

Classify sound attenuation for
services elements with the
appropriate part in the list below.
For example classify sound
attenuation for distribution
elements at G63.

G61 **Energy generation/storage/**
conversion
Classify the complete elements to
which these parts belong with
reference to Section G5, e.g.:
G61:G50 Energy generation/
storage/conversion for water
supply
G61:G52 Energy generation/
storage/conversion for HVAC
G61:G53 Energy generation/
storage/conversion for electric
power
1 Heat output
1 Heat generation
i.e. boilers (including fuel
storage), solar collectors.
2 Heat conversion
i.e. calorifiers, heat
exchangers.
2 Electricity output
1 Electricity generation
i.e. generators, turbines,
photovoltaic cells.
2 Electricity conversion
i.e. transformers, convertors.
3 Cooling output
4 Combined heat/power/cooling

G62 **Non-energy treatment/storage**
Classify the complete elements to
which these parts belong with
reference to Section G5.

G63 **Distribution**
Classify the complete elements to
which these parts belong with
reference to Section G5, e.g.:
G631:G52 Ductwork for HVAC
G632:G50 Pipework for water
supply
G632:G51 Pipework for gas
supply
1 Ductwork
2 Pipework
3 Cables
4 Pumps
5 Fans

G64 **Terminals**
Classify the complete elements to
which these parts belong with
reference to Section G5.

G65 **Package units**
Classify the complete elements to
which these parts belong with
reference to Section G5.

G66 Monitoring and control
Classify the complete elements to which these parts belong with reference to Section G5.

G69 Other parts of services elements

G7	External/site works

G71 Surface treatment
1 Hard surfaces
2 Landscaping

G72 Enclosure/division
1 Fencing/walling/hedges
2 Retaining walls

G73 Special purpose works
1 Water features, pools
2 Shelters, minor buildings
3 Bridges, underpasses
9 Other

G74 Fittings/furniture/equipment

G75 Mains supply
1 Water mains
2 Fire mains
3 Hot water/steam mains
4 Gas mains
5 Electric mains
6 Communications cable mains

G76 External distributed services
1 Lighting
2 Other

G77 Site/underground drainage

Elements for civil engineering works

Definition   **Element**: a major physical part or system of a building or other construction entity, which, in itself or in combination with other elements, fulfils a characteristic predominating function of the building or other construction entity. (Examples of characteristic predominating functions for civil engineering works are: supporting, enclosing or servicing.) Elements are considered without regard to the type of technical solution or the method or form of construction.

Examples   Foundations, abutments, piers, slopes, lighting services.

Use   Classifying design data, cost analyses and drawings of **construction entities other than** buildings.

For elements of buildings see Table G.

This table is not intended to be used for the classification of product information (see Table L).

Notes   "Civil engineering works" in Uniclass is equivalent to "construction entities other than buildings".

This table groups construction entities for civil engineering works so that ones which have similar elements appear in the same group. Within each group the common elements for the members of that group are listed. N.B. the groups in this table are the same as the groups in Table E Construction entities, except that Table E includes buildings.

The primary use for the table is expected to be cost analysis.

H1   Pavements and landscaping

Includes the structure of roads, runways and permanent ways for railways; also major soft landscaping works.
Where pavements and landscaping are a small item of work related to a construction entity in another category, classify in that other category.
For example classify road surfaces for bridges at H527; classify minor landscaping/planting associated with towers at H644.

H11   Site preparation
1 Site clearance
2 Ground contouring
3 Stabilisation

H12   Structure
1 Structural layers
    Includes base, sub-base.
2 Surfacing to pavements/hard landscaping
    Includes wearing surface, tracks, etc.
3 Edgework to pavements/hard landscaping
4 Planting/surfacing to major soft landscaping construction entities
    See also H143.

H13   Services
1 Mechanical engineering
2 Electrical installation
    1 Lighting
    2 Power
3 Communications
4 Protection
5 Drainage
9 Other services

H14   Ancillaries
1 Decoration
    Includes line painting, etc.
2 Fittings
    1 Track fittings
    2 Signs
    3 Gantries
    4 Street furniture
3 Minor landscaping/planting associated with roads, railways, etc.
    See also H124.
4 Enclosure, divisions
    Includes fences, barriers, etc.

H2   Tunnels, shafts, cuttings

H21   Site preparation
1 Site clearance
2 Ground contouring
3 Stabilisation

H22   Structure and tunnel formation
1 Shaft formation
2 Tunnel formation
3 Gallery formation
4 Permanent structural lining
5 Portals
6 Surfacing for transport

H23   Services
1 Mechanical engineering
2 Electrical installation
    1 Lighting
    2 Power
3 Communications
4 Protection
5 Drainage
9 Other services

H24   Ancillaries
1 Lining
2 Decoration
3 Fittings
4 Minor landscaping/planting
    See also H124.
5 Enclosure
    Includes barriers, guardrails, fences, etc.

H3   Embankments, retaining walls, etc.

H31   Site preparation
1 Site clearance
2 Ground contouring
3 Stabilisation

H32   Structure
1 Foundations
2 Major filling/embankments
3 Walls (non horizontal construction)
4 Slabs (horizontal construction)
5 Abutments
6 Sluices, channels, run-offs, etc.

H33   Services
1 Mechanical engineering
2 Electrical installation
    1 Lighting
    2 Power
3 Communications
4 Protection
5 Drainage
9 Other services

H34   Ancillaries
1 Fittings
    1 Signs
    2 Ancillary items
        Includes riprap etc.
2 Access
    Includes stairs, walkways
3 Minor landscaping/planting
    See also H124.
4 Enclosure
    Includes divisions, fencing, barriers, etc.

H4   Tanks, silos, etc.

H41   Site preparation
1 Site clearance
2 Ground contouring
3 Stabilisation

H42   Structure
1 Foundations
2 Walls
3 Slabs
    1 On ground
    2 Roof

H43   Services
1 Mechanical engineering
2 Electrical installation
    1 Lighting
    2 Power
3 Communications
4 Protection
5 Drainage
9 Other services

H44   Ancillaries
1 Decoration
2 Applied waterproofing
3 Fittings
4 Access
    Includes stairs, walkways.
5 Minor landscaping/planting
    See also H124.
6 Enclosure
    Includes barriers, guardrails, fences, etc.

H5	**Bridges, viaducts**

H51 Site preparation
1 Site clearance
2 Ground contouring
3 Stabilisation

H52 Structure
1 Foundations
2 Abutments
3 Piers
4 Towers (plus suspension/ stays)
5 Arches (plus suspension/ stays/struts)
6 Decks/slabs
7 Surfacing

H53 Services
1 Mechanical engineering
2 Electrical installation
   1 Lighting
   2 Power
3 Communications
4 Protection
5 Drainage
9 Other services

H54 Ancillaries
1 Decoration
2 Fittings
3 Access
   Includes stairs, walkways.
4 Minor landscaping/planting
   See also H124.
5 Enclosure
   Includes barriers, guardrails, fences, etc.

H6	**Towers, superstructures**

Excludes buildings.

H61 Site preparation
1 Site clearance
2 Ground contouring
3 Stabilisation

H62 Structure
1 Foundations
2 Slabs
3 Walls
4 Frame

H63 Services
1 Mechanical engineering
2 Electrical installation
   1 Lighting
   2 Power
3 Communications
4 Protection
5 Drainage
9 Other services

H64 Ancillaries
1 Decoration
2 Fittings
3 Access
   Includes stairs, walkways.
4 Minor landscaping/planting
   See also H124.
5 Enclosure
   Includes barriers, guardrails, fences, etc.

H7	**Pipelines, ducts, cables and channels**

i.e. linear constructions for carrying fluids, gases, electricity, electrical signals, etc.

H71 Site preparation
1 Site clearance
2 Ground contouring
3 Stabilisation

H72 The installation
1 Casing/outer lining of pipes, ducts, cables and channels
2 Inner lining
3 Inner cables, where present
4 Overground support
   e.g. pylons.
   For general information on pylons see E65.
5 Underground support
6 Terminals and junctions
   Includes inlets, outfalls, manholes, etc.
7 Pumps, other mechanical devices assisting the transportation/control of fluids and gases
8 Transformers, other electrical devices for transportation/ control of electricity and electrical signals
9 Insulation
   Where not covered by H721/3.

H73 Support services
1 Mechanical engineering
2 Electrical installation
   1 Lighting
   2 Power
3 Communications
4 Protection
5 Drainage
9 Other services

H74 Ancillaries
1 Unit enclosures
   Includes pump houses, transformer houses, etc.
2 Decoration
3 Fittings
4 Minor landscaping/planting
   See also H124.
5 Enclosure
   Includes barriers, guardrails, fences, etc.

Work sections for buildings

J

Definition

One or several physical parts of a building viewed as the result of particular skills and techniques applied to construction products and/or elements during the production phase.

Work sections are usually executed by particular types of subcontractor or groups of operatives. The class is influenced by both inputs (e.g. the construction products used) and outputs (the parts of the building or other structure constructed), and thus represents a dual concept.

Examples

Site survey, in situ concrete, glass block walling, curtain walling, warm air heating, lifts.

Use

Organising information in specifications and bills of quantities, classifying technical literature on particular construction operations. *This table is not intended to be used for the classification of product information (see Table L).*

Notes

This table is based on the *Common Arrangement of Work Sections for building works (CAWS)*. The letter J has been added to integrate CAWS into Uniclass, and this table includes the changes to be made for the first revision of CAWS, which is due to be published in late 1997. For use in specifications, bills of quantities or other project documents, please refer to the main CAWS publication; this classification version does not contain the details required for a thorough understanding and implementation of CAWS.

Concise Table

JA	Preliminaries/ General conditions		JW	Communications/Security/ Control systems
JB	Complete buildings/ structures/units		JX	Transport systems
JC	Existing site/buildings/ services		JY	Services reference specification
JD	Groundwork		JZ	Building fabric reference specification
JE	In situ concrete/ Large precast concrete			
JF	Masonry			
JG	Structural/Carcassing metal/ timber			
JH	Cladding/Covering			
JJ	Waterproofing			
JK	Linings/Sheathing/ Dry partitioning			
JL	Windows/Doors/Stairs			
JM	Surface finishes			
JN	Furniture/Equipment			
JP	Building fabric sundries			
JQ	Paving/Planting/Fencing/ Site furniture			
JR	Disposal systems			
JS	Piped supply systems			
JT	Mechanical heating/Cooling/ Refrigeration systems			
JU	Ventilation/Air conditioning systems			
JV	Electrical supply/power/ lighting systems			

JA Preliminaries/General conditions

JA1 The project generally
JA10 Project particulars
JA11 Documentation
JA12 The site/Existing buildings
JA13 Description of the work

JA2 The Contract
JA20 The Contract/Sub-contract

JA3 Employer's requirements
JA30 Tendering/Sub-letting/Supply
JA31 Provision, content and use of documents
JA32 Management of the Works
JA33 Quality standards/control
JA34 Security/Safety/Protection
JA35 Specific limitations on method/sequence/timing/use of site
JA36 Facilities/Temporary works/Services
JA37 Operation/Maintenance of the finished building

JA4 Contractor's general cost items
JA40 Management and staff
JA41 Site accommodation
JA42 Services and facilities
JA43 Mechanical plant
JA44 Temporary works

JA5 Work by others or subject to instruction
JA50 Work/Materials by the employer
JA51 Nominated sub-contractors
JA52 Nominated suppliers
JA53 Work by statutory authorities
JA54 Provisional work
JA55 Dayworks

JA6 Preliminaries for specialist contracts
JA60 Demolition contract preliminaries
JA61 Ground investigation contract preliminaries
JA62 Piling contract preliminaries
JA63 Landscape contract preliminaries

JA7 General specification for work packages
JA70 General specification for building fabric work
JA71 General specification for building services work

JB Complete buildings/structures/units

JB1 Prefabricated buildings/structures/units
JB10 Prefabricated buildings/structures
JB11 Prefabricated building units

JC Existing site/buildings/services

JC1 Investigations/Surveys
JC10 Site survey
JC11 Ground investigation
JC12 Underground services survey
JC13 Building fabric survey
JC14 Building services survey

JC2 Demolition/Removal
JC20 Demolition
JC21 Toxic/hazardous material removal

JC3 Alteration – support
JC30 Shoring/Facade retention

JC4 Repairing/Renovating/Conserving concrete/masonry
JC40 Cleaning masonry/concrete
JC41 Repairing/Renovating/Conserving masonry
JC42 Repairing/Renovating/Conserving concrete
JC45 Damp proof course renewal/insertion

JC5 Repairing/Renovating/Conserving metal/timber
JC50 Repairing/Renovating/Conserving metal
JC51 Repairing/Renovating/Conserving timber
JC52 Fungus/Beetle eradication

JC9 Alteration – composite items
JC90 Alterations – spot items

JD Groundwork

JD1 Ground stabilisation/dewatering
JD11 Soil stabilisation
JD12 Site dewatering

JD2 Excavation/filling
JD20 Excavating and filling
JD21 Landfill capping

JD3 Piling
JD30 Piling

JD4 Ground retention
JD40 Embedded retaining walls
JD41 Crib walls/Gabions/Reinforced earth

JD5 Underpinning
JD50 Underpinning

JE In situ concrete/Large precast concrete

JE0 Concrete construction generally
JE05 In situ concrete construction generally

JE1 Mixing/Casting/Curing/Spraying in situ concrete
JE10 Mixing/Casting/Curing in situ concrete
JE11 Sprayed concrete

JE2 Formwork
JE20 Formwork for in situ concrete

JE3 Reinforcement
JE30 Reinforcement for in situ concrete
JE31 Post tensioned reinforcement for in situ concrete

JE4 In situ concrete sundries
JE40 Designed joints in in situ concrete
JE41 Worked finishes/Cutting to in situ concrete
JE42 Accessories cast into in situ concrete

JE5 Structural precast concrete
JE50 Precast concrete frame structures

JE6 Composite construction
JE60 Precast/Composite concrete decking

JF Masonry

JF1 Brick/Block walling
JF10 Brick/Block walling
JF11 Glass block walling

JF2 Stone walling
JF20 Natural stone rubble walling
JF21 Natural stone ashlar walling/dressings
JF22 Cast stone walling/dressings

JF3 Masonry accessories
JF30 Accessories/Sundry items for brick/block/stone walling
JF31 Precast concrete sills/lintels/copings/features

JG Structural/Carcassing metal/timber

JG1 Structural/Carcassing metal
JG10 Structural steel framing
JG11 Structural aluminium framing
JG12 Isolated structural metal members

JG2 Structural/Carcassing timber
JG20 Carpentry/Timber framing/First fixing

JG3 Metal/Timber decking
JG30 Metal profiled sheet decking
JG31 Prefabricated timber unit decking
JG32 Edge supported/Reinforced woodwool slab decking

JH Cladding/Covering

JH1 Glazed cladding/covering
JH10 Patent glazing
JH11 Curtain walling
JH12 Plastics glazed vaulting/walling
JH13 Structural glass assemblies
JH14 Concrete rooflights/pavement lights
JH15 Rainscreen cladding/overcladding

JH2 Sheet/board cladding
JH20 Rigid sheet cladding
JH21 Timber weatherboarding

JH3 Profiled/flat sheet cladding/covering
JH30 Fibre cement profiled sheet cladding/covering
JH31 Metal profiled/flat sheet cladding/covering
JH32 Plastics profiled sheet cladding/covering
JH33 Bitumen and fibre profiled sheet cladding/covering

JH4 Panel cladding
JH40 Glass reinforced cement panel cladding/features
JH41 Glass reinforced plastics panel cladding/features
JH42 Precast concrete panel cladding/features
JH43 Metal panel cladding/features

JH5 Slab cladding
JH50 Precast concrete slab cladding/features
JH51 Natural stone slab cladding/features
JH52 Cast stone slab cladding/features

JH6 Slate/Tile cladding/covering
JH60 Plain roof tiling
JH61 Fibre cement slating
JH62 Natural slating
JH63 Reconstructed stone slating/tiling
JH64 Timber shingling
JH65 Single lap roof tiling
JH66 Bituminous felt shingling

JH7 Malleable sheet coverings/cladding
JH70 Malleable metal sheet pre-bonded coverings/claddings
JH71 Lead sheet coverings/flashings
JH72 Aluminium sheet coverings/flashings
JH73 Copper strip/sheet coverings/flashings
JH74 Zinc strip/sheet coverings/flashings
JH75 Stainless steel strip/sheet coverings/flashings
JH76 Fibre bitumen thermoplastic sheet coverings/flashings

JH9 Other cladding/covering
JH90 Tensile fabric coverings
JH91 Thatch roofing

JJ Waterproofing

JJ1 Cementitious coatings
JJ10 Specialist waterproof rendering

JJ2 Asphalt coatings
JJ20 Mastic asphalt tanking/damp proofing
JJ21 Mastic asphalt roofing/insulation/finishes
JJ22 Proprietary roof decking with asphalt finish

JJ3 Liquid applied coatings
JJ30 Liquid applied tanking/damp proofing
JJ31 Liquid applied waterproof roof coatings
JJ32 Sprayed vapour barriers
JJ33 In situ glass reinforced plastics

JJ4 Felt/flexible sheets
JJ40 Flexible sheet tanking/damp proofing
JJ41 Built-up felt roof coverings
JJ42 Single layer polymeric roof coverings
JJ43 Proprietary roof decking with felt finish
JJ44 Sheet linings for pools/lakes/waterways

JK Linings/Sheathing/Dry partitioning

JK1 Rigid sheet sheathing/linings
JK10 Plasterboard dry lining/partitions/ceilings
For panel partitions see JK30.
JK11 Rigid sheet flooring/sheathing/linings/casings
JK12 Under purlin/Inside rail panel linings
JK13 Rigid sheet fine linings/panelling
JK14 Glass reinforced gypsum linings/panelling/casings/mouldings
JK15 Vitreous enamel linings/panelling

JK2 Timber board/Strip linings
JK20 Timber board flooring/sheathing/linings/casings
JK21 Timber strip/board fine flooring/linings

JK3 Dry partitions
JK30 Panel partitions
JK31 *intentionally not used*
JK32 Framed panel cubicles
JK33 Concrete/Terrazzo
         partitions

JK4 False ceilings/floors
JK40 Demountable suspended
         ceilings
JK41 Raised access floors

JL	Windows/Doors/Stairs

**JL1 Windows/Rooflights/
          Screens/Louvres**
JL10 Windows
JL11 Rooflights/ Roof windows
JL12 Screens
JL13 Louvred ventilators
JL14 External louvres/
         shutters/canopies/blinds

JL2 Doors/Shutters/Hatches
JL20 Doors
JL21 Shutters
JL22 Hatches

JL3 Stairs/Walkways/Balustrades
JL30 Stairs/Walkways/
         Balustrades

JL4 Glazing
JL40 General glazing
JL41 Lead light glazing
JL42 Infill panels/sheets

JM	Surface finishes

JM1 Screeds/Trowelled flooring
JM10 Cement:sand/Concrete
         screeds/toppings
JM11 Mastic asphalt flooring/
         floor underlays
JM12 Trowelled bitumen/resin/
         rubber-latex flooring
JM13 Calcium sulfate based
         screeds

JM2 Plastered coatings
JM20 Plastered/Rendered/
         Roughcast coatings
JM21 Insulation with rendered
         finish
JM22 Sprayed monolithic
         coatings
JM23 Resin bound mineral
         coatings

**JM3 Work related to plastered
          coatings**
JM30 Metal mesh lathing/
         Anchored reinforcement
         for plastered coatings
JM31 Fibrous plaster

JM4 Rigid tiles
JM40 Stone/Concrete/Quarry/
         Ceramic tiling/Mosaic
JM41 Terrazzo tiling/In situ
         terrazzo
JM42 Wood block/Composition
         block/Parquet flooring

JM5 Flexible sheet/tile coverings
JM50 Rubber/Plastics/Cork/
         Lino/Carpet tiling/
         sheeting
JM51 Edge fixed carpeting
JM52 Decorative papers/fabrics

JM6 Painting
JM60 Painting/Clear finishing
JM61 Intumescent coatings for
         fire protection of
         steelwork

JN	Furniture/Equipment

**JN1 General purpose fixtures/
          furnishings/equipment**
JN10 General fixtures/
         furnishings/equipment
JN11 Domestic kitchen fittings
JN12 Catering equipment
JN13 Sanitary appliances/
         fittings
JN14 Plant containers
JN15 Signs/Notices

**JN2 Special purpose fixtures/
          furnishings/equipment**
JN20 Appropriate section title
         for each project
JN21 Appropriate section title
         for each project
JN22 Appropriate section title
         for each project
JN23 Appropriate section title
         for each project

JP	Building fabric sundries

JP1 Sundry proofing/insulation
JP10 Sundry insulation/
         proofing work/fire stops
JP11 Foamed/Fibre/Bead cavity
         wall insulation

JP2 Sundry finishes/fittings
JP20 Unframed isolated
         trims/skirtings/sundry
         items
JP21 Ironmongery
JP22 Sealant joints

**JP3 Sundry work in connection with
          engineering services**
JP30 Trenches/Pipeways/Pits
         for buried engineering
         services
JP31 Holes/Chases/Covers/
         Supports for services

JQ	Paving/Planting/Fencing/Site furniture

**JQ1 Edgings/Accessories for
          pavings**
JQ10 Kerbs/Edgings/Channels/
         Paving accessories

JQ2 Pavings
JQ20 Granular sub-bases to
         roads/pavings
JQ21 In situ concrete
         roads/pavings/bases
JQ22 Coated macadam/
         Asphalt roads/pavings
JQ23 Gravel/Hoggin/Bark
         roads/pavings
JQ24 Interlocking brick/block
         roads/pavings
JQ25 Slab/Brick/Sett/Cobble
         pavings
JQ26 Special surfacings/
         pavings for sport/general
         amenity

JQ3 Planting
JQ30 Seeding/Turfing
JQ31 Planting
JQ32 Planting in special
         environments
JQ35 Landscape maintenance

JQ4 Fencing
JQ40 Fencing

JQ5 Site furniture
JQ50 Site/Street furniture/
         equipment

Work sections for buildings

JR Disposal systems

JR1 Drainage
JR10 Rainwater pipework/gutters
JR11 Foul drainage above ground
JR12 Drainage below ground
JR13 Land drainage
JR14 Laboratory/Industrial waste drainage

JR2 Sewerage
JR20 Sewage pumping
JR21 Sewage treatment/sterilisation

JR3 Refuse disposal
JR30 Centralised vacuum cleaning
JR31 Refuse chutes
JR32 Compactors/Macerators
JR33 Incineration plant

JS Piped supply systems

JS1 Water supply
JS10 Cold water
JS11 Hot water
JS12 Hot and cold water (small scale)
JS13 Pressurised water
JS14 Irrigation
JS15 Fountains/Water features

JS2 Treated on site water supply
JS20 Treated/Deionised/Distilled water
JS21 Swimming pool water treatment

JS3 Gas supply
JS30 Compressed air
JS31 Instrument air
JS32 Natural gas
JS33 Liquefied petroleum gas
JS34 Medical/Laboratory gas

JS4 Petrol/Oil storage
JS40 Petrol/Diesel storage/distribution
JS41 Fuel oil storage/distribution

JS5 Other supply systems
JS50 Vacuum
JS51 Steam

JS6 Fire fighting – water
JS60 Fire hose reels
JS61 Dry risers
JS62 Wet risers
JS63 Sprinklers
JS64 Deluge
JS65 Fire hydrants

JS7 Fire fighting – gas/foam
JS70 Gas fire fighting
JS71 Foam fire fighting

JT Mechanical heating/Cooling/Refrigeration systems

JT1 Heat source
JT10 Gas/Oil fired boilers
JT11 Coal fired boilers
JT12 Electrode/Direct electric boilers
JT13 Packaged steam generators
JT14 Heat pumps
JT15 Solar collectors
JT16 Alternative fuel boilers

JT2 Primary heat distribution
JT20 Primary heat distribution

JT3 Heat distribution/utilisation – water
JT30 Medium temperature hot water heating
JT31 Low temperature hot water heating
JT32 Low temperature hot water heating (small scale)
JT33 Steam heating

JT4 Heat distribution/utilisation – air
JT40 Warm air heating
JT41 Warm air heating (small scale)
JT42 Local heating units

JT5 Heat recovery
JT50 Heat recovery

JT6 Central refrigeration/Distribution
JT60 Central refrigeration plant
JT61 Chilled water

JT7 Local cooling/Refrigeration
JT70 Local cooling units
JT71 Cold rooms
JT72 Ice pads

JU Ventilation/Air conditioning systems

JU1 Ventilation/Fume extract
JU10 General ventilation
JU11 Toilet ventilation
JU12 Kitchen ventilation
JU13 Car parking ventilation
JU14 Smoke extract/Smoke control
JU15 Safety cabinet/Fume cupboard extract
JU16 Fume extract
JU17 Anaesthetic gas extract

JU2 Industrial extract
JU20 Dust collection

JU3 Air conditioning – all air
JU30 Low velocity air conditioning
JU31 VAV air conditioning
JU32 Dual-duct air conditioning
JU33 Multi-zone air conditioning

JU4 Air conditioning – air/water
JU40 Induction air conditioning
JU41 Fan-coil air conditioning
JU42 Terminal re-heat air conditioning
JU43 Terminal heat pump air conditioning

JU5 Air conditioning – hybrid
JU50 Hybrid system air conditioning

JU6 Air conditioning – local
JU60 Air conditioning units

JU7 Other air systems
JU70 Air curtains

JV Electrical supply/power/lighting systems

JV1 Generation/Supply/HV distribution
JV10 Electricity generation plant
JV11 HV supply/distribution/public utility supply
JV12 LV supply/public utility supply

JV2 General LV distribution/lighting/power
JV20 LV distribution
JV21 General lighting
JV22 General LV power

JV3 Special types of supply/distribution
JV30 Extra low voltage supply
JV31 DC supply
JV32 Uninterrupted power supply

JV4 Special lighting
JV40 Emergency lighting
JV41 Street/Area/Flood lighting
JV42 Studio/Auditorium/Arena lighting

JV5 Electric heating
JV50 Electric underfloor/ceiling heating
JV51 Local electric heating units

JV9 General/Other electrical work
JV90 General lighting and power (small scale)

JW Communications/Security/ Control systems

JW1 Communications – speech/ audio
JW10 Telecommunications
JW11 Paging/Emergency call
JW12 Public address/ Conference audio facilities

JW2 Communications – audio-visual
JW20 Radio/TV/CCTV
JW21 Projection
JW22 Information/Advertising display
JW23 Clocks

JW3 Communications – data
JW30 Data transmission

JW4 Security
JW40 Access control
JW41 Security detection and alarm

JW5 Protection
JW50 Fire detection and alarm
JW51 Earthing and bonding
JW52 Lightning protection
JW53 Electromagnetic screening
JW54 Liquid detection alarm
JW55 Gas detection alarm
JW56 Electronic bird/vermin control

JW6 Central control
JW60 Central control/Building management

JX Transport systems

JX1 People/Goods
JX10 Lifts
JX11 Escalators
JX12 Moving pavements
JX13 Powered stairlifts
JX14 Fire escape chutes/slings

JX2 Goods/Maintenance
JX20 Hoists
JX21 Cranes
JX22 Travelling cradles/ Gantries/Ladders
JX23 Goods distribution/ Mechanised warehousing

JX3 Documents
JX30 Mechanical document conveying
JX31 Pneumatic document conveying
JX32 Automatic document filing and retrieval

JY Services reference specification

JY1 Pipelines and ancillaries
JY10 Pipelines
JY11 Pipeline ancillaries

JY2 General pipeline equipment
JY20 Pumps
JY21 Water tanks/cisterns
JY22 Heat exchangers
JY23 Storage cylinders/ Calorifiers
JY24 Trace heating
JY25 Cleaning and chemical treatment

JY3 Air ductlines and ancillaries
JY30 Air ductlines/ancillaries

JY4 General air ductline equipment
JY40 Air handling units
JY41 Fans
JY42 Air filtration
JY43 Heating/Cooling coils
JY44 Air treatment
JY45 Silencers/Acoustic treatment
JY46 Grilles/Diffusers/Louvres

JY5 Other common mechanical items
JY50 Thermal insulation
JY51 Testing and commissioning of mechanical services
JY52 Vibration isolation mountings
JY53 Control components – mechanical
JY54 Identification – mechanical
JY59 Sundry common mechanical items

JY6 Cables and wiring
JY60 Conduit and cable trunking
JY61 HV/LV cables and wiring
JY62 Busbar trunking
JY63 Support components – cables

JY7 General electrical equipment
JY70 HV switchgear
JY71 LV switchgear and distribution boards
JY72 Contactors and starters
JY73 Luminaires and lamps
JY74 Accessories for electrical services

JY8 Other common electrical items
JY80 Earthing and bonding components
JY81 Testing and commissioning of electrical services
JY82 Identification – electrical
JY89 Sundry common electrical items

JY9 Other common mechanical and/or electrical items
JY90 Fixing to building fabric
JY91 Off-site painting/Anti-corrosion treatments
JY92 Motor drives – electric

JZ Building fabric reference specification

JZ1 Fabricating
JZ10 Purpose made joinery
JZ11 Purpose made metalwork
JZ12 Preservative/Fire retardant treatments for timber

JZ2 Fixing/Jointing
JZ20 Fixings/Adhesives
JZ21 Mortars
JZ22 Sealants

JZ3 Finishing
JZ30 Off-site painting
JZ31 Powder coatings
JZ32 Liquid coatings
JZ33 Anodising

Work sections for civil engineering works

K

Definition

One or several physical parts of civil engineering works viewed as the result of particular skills and techniques applied to construction products and/or elements during the production phase.

Work sections are usually executed by particular types of subcontractor or groups of operatives. The class is influenced by both inputs (e.g. the construction products used) and outputs (the parts of the building or other structure constructed), and thus represents a dual concept.

Examples

Soil stabilisation, dredging, pipework, metalwork, piling, road surfacing, tunnel lining.

Use

Organising information in specifications and bills of quantities, classifying technical literature on particular construction operations. *This table is not intended to be used for the classification of product information (see Table L).*

Notes

This table is based on the Civil Engineering Standard Method of Measurement, third edition (CESMM3). It is intended only as a guide to filing information on work sections for civil engineering works. For project use the full version of CESMM3 should be used.

Concise Table

KA	General items		KW	Waterproofing
KB	Ground investigation		KX	Miscellaneous work
KC	Geotechnical and other specialist processes		KY	Sewer renovation and ancillary work
KD	Demolition and site clearance		KZ	Simple building works
KE	Earthworks			
KF	In situ concrete			
KG	Concrete ancillaries			
KH	Precast concrete			
KI	Pipework – pipes			
KJ	Pipework – fittings and valves			
KK	Pipework – manholes and pipework ancillaries			
KL	Pipework – laying and excavation ancillaries			
KM	Structural metalwork			
KN	Miscellaneous metalwork			
KO	Timber			
KP	Piles			
KQ	Piling ancillaries			
KR	Roads and paving			
KS	Rail track			
KT	Tunnels			
KU	Brickwork, blockwork and masonry			
KV	Painting			

KA General items

Includes:
General obligations, site services and facilities, temporary works, testing of materials and work, provisional sums, prime cost items, performance bonds, insurance of the works, third party insurance, daywork.

KB Ground investigation

Includes:
Trial pits and trenches, boreholes, samples, site and laboratory tests, professional services in connection with ground investigation.

KC Geotechnical and other specialist processes

Includes:
Geotechnical processes for altering the properties of soils and rocks.

KD Demolition and site clearance

Includes:
Demolition and removal of natural and artificial articles, objects and obstructions which are above the Original Surface.

Excludes:
Removal of articles, objects and materials at or below the Original Surface.

KE Earthworks

Includes:
Excavation, dredging, filling, compaction, disposal and landscaping.

Excludes:
Excavation for diaphragm walls, pipes and sewers, pointing, piles, tunnels, foundations for traffic signals, fences which are included in relevant classes.

KF In situ concrete

Excludes:
In situ concrete for capping boreholes, diaphragm walls, granolithic and applied finishes, drainage and pipework, piles, roads and pavings, tunnels, foundations for fences which are included in relevant classes.

KG Concrete ancillaries

Includes:
Formwork, reinforcement, joints for in situ concrete, post-tensioned prestressing, concrete accessories.

KH Precast concrete

Includes:
Manufacture, erection, joining and fixing of precast concrete units.

Excludes:
Post-tensioned prestressing, precast concrete pipework, manholes, gullies, piles, paving, tunnel linings, blockwork fencing which are included in relevant classes.

KI Pipework – pipes

Includes:
Provision, laying and jointing of pipework, excavation and backfilling pipe trenches.

Excludes:
Pipes building services which are included in class KZ.

KJ Pipework – fittings and valves

KK Pipework – manholes and pipework ancillaries

Includes:
Manholes and other chambers, ducts, culverts, crossing and reinstatement.

Excludes:
Ducted building services which are included in class KZ.

KL Pipework – laying and excavation ancillaries

Pipework – supports and protection, ancillaries to laying and excavation.

Includes:
Extras to excavation and backfilling of trenches for pipework, ducts and metal culverts, manholes and other chambers, headings, thrust boring and pipe jacking. Pipe laying in headings and by thrust boring and pipe jacking, provision of supports and protection to pipework, ducts and metal culverts.

Excludes:
Insulation to building services which are included in class KZ.

K

Work sections for civil engineering works

KM Structural metalwork

Excludes:
Metalwork in concrete, pipework, piles, fences and miscellaneous metalwork which are included in relevant classes.

KN Miscellaneous metalwork

Includes:
Miscellaneous metalwork to stairways, platforms, bridge parapets, flooring, cladding, duct covers, bridge bearings, tanks.

Excludes:
Metal reinforcement or inserts in concrete, pipework, structural metalwork, timber fittings and fasteners, piles, traffic signs, rail track fences which are included in relevant classes.

KO Timber

Includes:
Timber components and fittings, timber decking, fittings and fasteners to timber components and decking.

Excludes:
Formwork to concrete, timber piles, timber sleepers, timber supports in tunnels, timber fencing, carpentry and simple joinery in building works incidental to civil engineering works which are included in relevant classes.

KP Piles

Includes:
Bored or driven cast in place concrete piles, preformed concrete piles, timber piles, steel piles (interlocking or isolated).

Excludes:
Borings for site investigation, ground anchors, walings and tie rods, piling ancillaries which are included in relevant classes.

KQ Piling ancillaries

Includes:
Works ancillary to piling.

Excludes:
Ground anchors piles, walings and tie rods which are included in relevant classes.

KR Roads and paving

Includes:
Sub-base, base and surfacing of roads, runways and other paved area, kerbings and light duty pavements, footways and cycle tracks, traffic signs and markings.

Excludes:
Earthworks, drainage, fences and gates, gantries and other substantial structures supporting traffic signs, maintenance of roads and pavings which are included in relevant classes.

KS Rail track

Includes:
Track foundations, rails, sleepers, fittings, switches and crossings.

Excludes:
Overhead crane rails, concrete track foundations which are included in relevant classes.

KT Tunnels

Includes:
Excavation, lining and securing of tunnels, shafts and other subterranean cavities.

Excludes:
Geotechnical processes carried out from the ground surface, reinforcement to in situ lining, pipe laying in headings, tunnels and shafts, cut and cover tunnels which are included in relevant classes.

KU Brickwork, blockwork and masonry

Excludes:
Brickwork in manholes and other brickwork incidental to pipework, brickwork in sewer renovation which are included in relevant classes.

KV Painting

Includes:
In situ painting.

Excludes:
Painting carried out prior to delivery of components to the site.

KW   Waterproofing

Includes:
Damp proofing, tanking and roofing.

Excludes:
Waterproofing joints, damp proof courses in brickwork, blockwork and masonry, surface finishes and linings to simple building works incidental to civil engineering works which are included in relevant classes.

KX   Miscellaneous work

Includes:
Fences, gates and their foundations; drainage to structures above ground; rock filled gabions.

KY   Sewer renovation and ancillary work

Includes:
Preparation and renovation of existing sewers and water mains; new manholes within the length of existing sewers; work to existing manholes.

Excludes:
Grouting carried out from outside the sewer; new pipework, new fittings and valves used in water main renovation; extras to excavation and backfilling for new manholes and other chambers which are included in relevant classes.

KZ   Simple building works

Simple building works incidental to civil engineering works.

Includes:
Carpentry and joinery, insulation, windows, doors and glazing, surface finishes, linings and partitions, piped, ducted or cabled building services.

Construction products

L

Definition
Products, components and "kits of parts" incorporated or intended for incorporation into buildings or other constructions, including furniture and fixtures.

For construction plant and equipment see Table M Construction aids.

Examples
Culverts, traffic signals, space frames, lintels, bricks, supply pumps, washbasins, solar collectors, lifts, office furniture.

Use
Design and/or technical information relating to construction products. While primarily intended for trade literature, price lists and the like, it can also be used for organising information/standards from trade associations and third party certification schemes (BSI Kitemark, British Board of Agrément, etc.).

Concise Table

L1 Ground treatment and retention products

L11 Ground anchorages
L12 Ground improvement
L13 Land/field drainage
L14 Sheeting, revetments
L15 Land/water retention products
L16 Slide/avalanche protection products

L2 Complete construction entities and components

L21 Civil engineering works products
L22 System buildings, minor buildings, room units

L3 Structural and space division products

L31 Foundation products
L32 Masonry
L33 In situ concrete
L34 Structural precast concrete
L35 Structural metal
L36 Structural timber
L37 Structural components in other materials
L38 Non-structural space division products

L4 Access, barrier and circulation products

L41 Doors, windows, etc. (access products)
L42 Protection of openings
L43 Circulation/escape
L44 Barriers
L45 Ancillary access, barrier and circulation products

L5 Coverings, claddings, linings

L51 Wall coverings, claddings, linings
L52 Roof coverings, claddings, linings
L53 Floor coverings, claddings, linings
L54 Ceiling coverings, claddings
L55 General products for coverings and claddings

L6 General purpose civil engineering and construction fabric products

L61 Loose granular fills, aggregates, chips
L62 Binding agents
L63 Admixtures, additives
L64 Mortars
L65 General purpose sections
L66 General purpose sheets
L67 General purpose fixing/jointing products
L68 Proofings, insulation, paints, etc.
L69 General cleaning products

L7 Services

L71 Supply/storage/distribution of liquids and gases
L72 Sanitary, laundry, cleaning equipment
L73 Waste handling equipment
L74 Electric power and lighting services products
L75 Climate control plant and equipment (HVAC)
L76 Information/communication services products
L77 Transport services products
L78 General purpose and ancillary services products

L8 Fixtures and furnishings

L81 External furniture and fittings
L82 Domestic and general furniture and fittings
L83 Catering furniture
L84 Educational, cultural, display furniture, fittings
L85 Work environment furniture, fittings
L86 Communication fittings
L87 Furnishings, ornaments, internal decoration
L88 Portable fire suppression systems
L89 Furniture accessories

L1 Ground treatment and retention products

L11 Ground anchorages

L111 Rock anchorages, rock bolts

L112 Plate anchors

L113 Grouted anchors

L114 Soil nails

L115 Parts of ground anchorages
1 Anchor heads
2 Tendons

L12 Ground improvement

L121 Chemical soil stabilisation products
1 Injectable resinous soil stabilisation products

L122 Fill blocks

L123 Compressible fill

L13 Land/field drainage

See L2123 for drainage associated with roads/runways, including culverts.

L131 Complete field drain systems

L132 Field drain components

L14 Sheeting, revetments

L141 Geosynthetics
1 Geotextiles
2 Geogrids
3 Geocomposites
4 Geomembranes
   1 Separating membranes
   2 Filter membranes
   3 Gas barrier membranes
5 Bentonite clay liners

L142 Revetments
Excludes geosynthetics.
1 Soil blankets
2 Trench revetments
   1 Trench supports
   2 Trench sheeting

L15 Land/water retention products

L151 Sheet piles
See also L314.

L152 Diaphragm walls, slurry walls

L153 Precast concrete retaining units

L154 Crib walls

L155 Gabions

L156 Fascines

L157 Dykes/banks

L16 Slide/avalanche protection products

L2 Complete construction entities and components

L21 Civil engineering works products

L211 Bridge products
01 Complete bridge systems
02 Bridge beams
03 Wire ropes for suspension bridges
   Includes fittings.
04 Bridge decking
05 Bridge deck waterproofing
06 Anti skid texturing
07 Bridge drainage units
08 Bridge parapets
09 Bearings
10 Shock absorbers
11 Expansion joints

L212 Road/runway products
1 Entire roads/runways (portable roadways)
2 Road/runway surfacings
3 Road/runway drainage
   Small scale channels, gullies are at L7315.
   1 Culverts
      1 Complete culvert systems
      2 Culvert components
   2 Road/runway gullies
   3 Road/runway channels
      1 Filter drains and channels
   9 Other road/runway drainage products
4 Ancillary products for runways/air transport
   1 Helicopter landing pads
   2 Other air transport products
5 Ancillary products for roads
   1 Kerbs
   2 Road humps
   3 Guardrails
   4 Crash barriers
   5 Cattle grids
   6 Noise barriers

L213 Railway products
1 Complete railway systems
2 Sleepers
3 Rails
4 Platform units
5 Platform copings
9 Other railway components

L214 Cable transport
1 Cable ways
   Includes gondola and car cable ways.
2 Chair lifts
3 Ski-lifts

L

L215 Transport control and monitoring products
1 Road signs
   Pedestrian signs are at L81112.
   1 Illuminated road signs
2 Traffic lights
3 Parking equipment
   1 Parking meters
   2 Pay and display machines
   9 Other
4 Speed cameras
5 Other road control and monitoring products
   1 Verge markers
      Bollards are at L81101.
   2 Road mirrors
   3 Road studs
6 Railway signals
7 Navigation signals
8 Aviation signals and monitoring
   1 Ground lighting
   2 Approach indicators
   3 Aviation monitoring equipment

L216 Water engineering construction products

1 Inland waters construction products
   1 Canal locks
      1 Complete canal locks
      2 Canal lock components
   2 Reservoir components
   3 Dams
      1 Complete dams
      2 Dam components
   4 Spillways
      1 Complete spillways
      2 Spillway components
   5 Weir components
   6 Barrages
      1 Complete barrages
      2 Barrage components

2 Coastline and maritime works products
   1 Floating docks
      1 Complete floating dock systems
      2 Floating dock components
   2 Loading ramps
      1 Complete loading ramp systems
      2 Loading ramp components
   3 Pontoons
      1 Complete pontoon systems
      2 Pontoon components
   4 Jetties
      1 Complete jetty systems
      2 Jetty components
   5 Breakwater products
      1 Tetrapods
      9 Other breakwater products

L217 Public health and environmental engineering products

1 Water supply products, large scale/municipal/mains
   Local/small scale water supply products are at L711.
   1 Water treatment products
      1 Desalination plant products
      2 Tanks, filters, etc. for treatment
      3 Chlorination products
      4 Deionisation/distillation products
   2 Water distribution systems products
      1 Water mains
      2 Booster pumps
      3 Service reservoirs
         Other reservoir components are at L21612.

2 Sewerage and drainage system products, large scale/municipal/mains
   Local/small scale sewerage and drainage system products are at L731.
   1 Pipes for sewers and drains
   2 Detention/stormwater retention tanks
   3 Connectors
   4 Manholes/inspection chambers
      1 Manhole covers
      2 Manhole frames
   5 Grease traps/petrol interceptors
   6 Rodding points
   9 Other products for sewers and drains

3 Sewage treatment products
   See L7317 for local sewage storage and treatment products, including septic tanks and cesspools.
   1 Traps, screens
   2 Tanks, filters, etc. for treatment
   3 Sewage pumps

4 Refuse disposal plant
   Local solid waste handling products are at L732.
   1 Incinerators
      Includes incinerators for clinical waste, sanitary waste.
   2 Crushers
   3 Compactors/packagers
   4 Baling presses

5 Transmission networks

6 Pollution monitoring and control products

L218 Specialised superstructures
1 Industrial chimneys
   Flues and chimneys are at L7332.
   1 Complete chimneys
   2 Chimney components
      1 Chimney shafts
      2 Chimney linings
2 Towers
   1 Cooling towers
      Large scale, as part of power stations.
      Small scale HVAC cooling towers are at L7529.
   2 Water towers
      Large scale water tanks are at L2191.
      1 Complete water towers
      2 Water tower components
   9 Other towers
3 Masts
   1 Complete masts
   2 Mast components
4 Gantries
   1 Complete gantries
   2 Gantry components

L219 Storage constructions
1 Tanks
   e.g. large scale water tanks.
   1 Complete tanks
   2 Tank components
2 Silos
   1 Complete silos
   2 Silo components
3 Bunkers
   1 Complete bunkers
   2 Bunker components
4 Gasholders
   1 Complete gasholders
   2 Gasholder components

L22 System buildings, minor buildings, room units

Includes volumetric buildings.

L221 Complete buildings, portable buildings
01 System built houses
02 System buildings other than houses
03 Indoor system buildings
04 Inflatable buildings
05 Shelters
   For bus shelters see L81113.
06 Greenhouses, glasshouses
07 Sanitary and body care buildings
08 Funerary constructions
09 Summerhouses
   Includes gazebos, pavilions, belvederes.
10 Emergency shelters
11 Kiosks

Construction products

L222 **Room units, space enclosing parts**
1 General purpose room units
2 Storage room units
3 Sanitary and body care room units
4 Controlled environment rooms
  1 Coldrooms/coldstores
  2 Clean rooms
  3 Electromagnetically shielded rooms
  4 X-ray shielded rooms
5 Plant and control room units
6 Non-structural cubicles
7 Corridor units
8 Conservatories
9 Car ports, garages

L3 Structural and space division products

L31 Foundation products

L311 **Pad foundations**

L312 **Raft foundations**

L313 **Strip foundations**
Includes blocks for strip foundations.

L314 **Piles**
Excludes sheet piles – see L151.
1 Driven piles
  1 Driven cast-in-place piles
  2 Precast piles
  3 Steel piles
  4 Timber piles
    L31415/8
    Parts of driven piles
  5 Casing
  6 Core/mandrels
  7 Shoes
  8 Helmets
2 Bored piles
  1 Lining/casing
3 Screw piles

L315 **Caissons**

L316 **Columns bases**

L317 **Foundation instrumentation**

L32 Masonry

L321 **Bricks**
1 Clay bricks
  1 Common
  2 Facing
  3 Engineering
  4 Fire/refractory bricks
  5 Radiation shielding bricks
  6 Glazed bricks
  9 Other types
2 Concrete bricks
  1 Common
  2 Facing
  9 Other types
3 Calcium silicate bricks
  1 Common
  2 Facing
  9 Other types

L322 **Blocks**
1 Dense concrete blocks
  1 Common
  2 Facing
  3 Screen walling blocks
  4 Glazed blocks
2 Reconstructed stone blocks
3 Lightweight/insulated blocks
  1 Lightweight aggregate concrete blocks
  2 Aerated concrete blocks
  3 Insulated blocks
4 Hollow clay blocks
5 Glass blocks

L323 **Stone**
Reconstructed stone blocks are at L3222.
1 Rubble stone
2 Dressed/ashlar stone

L324 **Dressings**
1 Lintels (which function as dressings)
  For inner leaf lintels see L325.
2 Sills
3 Copings
4 Quoins
5 Cornices

L325 **Lintels (other than dressings)**

L326 **Fixings**
These are special fixings which are essential to the structural integrity of masonry. For general purpose fixings see L671.
1 Brackets etc. for supporting brickwork
2 Wall connectors
3 Wall ties and cramps
9 Other special masonry fixings

L327 **Ancillary products**
1 Cavity trays
2 Cavity closers
3 Cavity ventilation units
4 Air bricks

L33 In situ concrete

L331 **Ready mixed concrete**

L332 **Permanent formwork**
Temporary formwork is at M2.
1 Profiled steel structural formwork
2 Non-structural formwork

L333 **Reinforcement**
Fibre reinforcement is at L633.
1 Reinforcement cages
2 Steel bars
3 Steel mesh
4 Couplers
5 Spacers/chairs

L334 Prestressing components
1 Steel cables
2 Steel bars
3 Glassfibre tendons
4 Other types of tendons
5 Couplers
6 Cable troughs
7 Anchorages
9 Other

L335 Cast-in jointing
1 Crack inducers
2 Waterbars

L336 Ancillary products
For fixings for in situ concrete see L671 General purpose fixings. However, structural engineers may wish to classify cast-in fixings here.

L34 Structural precast concrete

L341 Complete frames

L342 Structural decks and slabs
1 Slabs
2 Joists and infill blocks
3 Planks

L343 Structural beams and columns
1 Beams
2 Columns

L344 Other structural components

L345 Fixings and ancillary products
1 Fixings
These include special fixings which are essential to the structural integrity of precast concrete structures. For general purpose fixings see L671.

L35 Structural metal

Metal joists, sections, etc. are at L6512.

L351 Complete frames

L352 Fabricated components
1 Castellated sections
2 Curved sections
3 Trusses
4 Lattice joists
5 Space frames/decks
9 Other fabricated components

L353 Fixings and ancillary products
1 Fixings
These include special fixings which are essential to the structural integrity of metal structures. For general purpose fixings see L671.
  1 Bolts

L36 Structural timber

Timber sections etc. are at L6511.

L361 Complete frames
1 Conventional timber frames
2 Glulam frames

L362 Fabricated components
1 Trussed rafters
2 Timber/plywood fabricated beams
3 Glulam beams
9 Other fabricated components

L363 Fixings and ancillary products
1 Fixings
These include special fixings which are essential to the structural integrity of timber structures. For general purpose fixings see L671.
  1 Nail plates
  2 Bolts
  3 Joist hangers/connectors

L37 Structural components in other materials

e.g. GRP structural components.

L38 Non-structural space division products

In any material.

L381 Facades and roofs
1 Curtain walls
Includes panels, accessories.
2 Patent glazing
3 Structural glazing
4 Combined door and screen units
Includes entrance screens and shopfronts.

L382 Prefabricated roof forms
1 Folded plate roofs
2 Curved shell roofs
Includes domes, cupolas, barrel, hyperbolic paraboloid.
3 Other roof shapes
Includes spires.
4 Over-roofing systems

L383 Tensile fabric structures

L384 Partitions, non-structural internal walls

L385 Room dividers

L386 Access floors

L387 Suspended ceilings
Includes accessories, e.g. cavity barriers, panels.

L388 Balcony units

L4 Access, barrier and circulation products

L41 Doors, windows, etc. (access products)

L411 Doors
Includes door assemblies, garage doors, patio doors, french windows, etc.

L41101/10
By method of opening
01 Side hung
02 Revolving
03 Sliding
04 Sliding/folding
05 Rolling up
06 Stacking
07 Overhead
08 Flexible
09 Automatic
10 Half doors

L41121/24
By purpose
21 Firedoors
22 Security doors
23 Controlled environment doors
24 Acoustic doors

L412 Hatches

L413 Windows
By method of opening; includes window assemblies.
01 Fixed
02 Side-hung casement
03 Top-hung casement
04 Bottom-hung casement
05 Horizontal sliding
06 Vertical sliding
07 Sliding projecting
08 Horizontal pivot
09 Vertical pivot
10 Tilt and turn
11 Louvre
12 Sash

L414 Rooflights
Includes burglar resistant rooflights, and rooflights by shape, e.g. domelights.
1 Individual units
2 Continuous units
3 Dormers
4 Northlights
5 Skylights
6 Lantern lights

L415 Pavement lights

L416 Trap doors

L418 Ancillary products for doors and windows, architectural ironmongery

1 Door furniture
   Includes emergency exit hardware; letters and numerals are at L8457.
   1 Door openers
   2 Door closers
   3 Knobs, levers, handles
   4 Roses, escutcheons
   5 Fingerplates, kick plates
   6 Knockers
   7 Letter boxes/plates
   8 Locks
      1 Mortice locks
      2 Latches
      3 Deadlocks
      4 Electric/electronic locks
      5 Padlocks
      6 Knobsets
   9 Bolts
      1 Barrel bolts
      2 Flush bolts
      3 Mortice bolts
      4 Indicator bolts
      5 Espagnolette, cremorne bolts
      6 Panic bolts, emergency exit hardware

2 Window furniture
   1 Fasteners, stays, hooks
   2 Locks, catches, bolts
   3 Handles
   4 External louvres
   5 Internal louvres

3 Hinges
   01 Butt hinges
   02 Parliament hinges
   03 Lift-off hinges
   04 Ball bearing hinges
   05 Bolt hinges
   06 Tee (cross-garnet) hinges
   07 Counter flap hinges, strap-hinges, angle hinges
   08 Blade hinges
   09 Spring hinges
   10 Fully reversible hinges

4 Architraves

5 Security bars

6 Films applied to glass
   1 Solar control film
   2 Shatter resistant film
      Includes blast protection film.
   3 Tinted/opaque film

7 Ventilators/condensation controls/glazing channels
   1 Trickle vents

8 Thresholds, sills

9 Weatherbars, weatherseals, draught excluders

L42 Protection of openings

L421 Overhanging screens
1 Canopies
2 Awnings
3 Non-structural porches etc.
   1 Porches
   2 Porticos
   3 Door canopies, surrounds
   4 Overdoors
      Includes ancillary external doors, such as decorative ironwork grilles or flyscreens.

L422 Blinds
1 Blackout blinds
2 Insect screens
3 Roller blinds
4 Venetian blinds
5 Vertical blinds

L423 Shutters
1 Fire/smoke shutters
   1 Firebreak shutters
   2 Escalator shutters
2 Internal shutters
3 Security shutters
4 Industrial shutters

L424 Grilles
1 Roller grilles

L43 Circulation/escape

L431 Flat circulation
1 Ramps
   1 Collapsible ramps
2 Walkways, elevated walkways
   1 Footbridges

L432 Stepped circulation
1 Ladders (fixed)
   1 Access ladders
   2 Loft ladders
   3 Roll-up ladders
   4 Sliding ladders
2 Stairs
   1 Straight stairs
   2 Curved stairs
   3 Spiral stairs
   4 Stair parts
      1 Nosings
      2 Inserts
      3 Treads

L433 Means of escape in case of fire
1 Fire escapes/stairs
2 Fire ladders
3 Slings
4 Escape slides

L   Construction products

L44 Barriers

L441 Enclosures
1 Fences
2 Gates

L442 Circulation guiding and safety
1 Railings
Includes balustrades, infill panels.
2 Hand rails, grab rails
Includes hand rail caps.

L443 Anti-intruder barriers
1 Barbed wire
2 Razor tape
3 Spikes

L444 Vehicle barriers
Bollards are at L81101.

L45 Ancillary access, barrier and circulation products

L451 Turnstiles

L452 Door entry token systems

L453 Programmable ticketing entry systems

L454 Door remote control units

L5 Coverings, claddings, linings

L51 Wall coverings, claddings, linings

Includes coverings mainly for walls, but occasionally for other elements.

L511 Wall cladding sections
1 Weatherboarding
Includes clapboards, shiplap.

L512 Wall tiles
Includes brick slips.
1 Mosaic
Includes mosaic for use on floors or elsewhere.

L513 Wall cladding panels, slabs; facing slabs
1 Stone sheets
Includes marble sheets.

L514 Wall cladding, lining sheet materials
1 Wall cladding sheets
Roof and wall cladding sheets see L5221.

L515 Wall coverings
1 Paper and vinyl
2 Textile
3 Other
Includes leather and cork.

L516 Wall linings
1 Wall panelling

L517 Wall finishing coatings
Plaster is at L551.
1 Renders
  1 Pebbledash
  2 Rough cast

L519 Ancillary products for wall coverings, claddings, linings
1 Fixings
2 Skirting boards

L52 Roof coverings, claddings, linings

Includes coverings mainly for roofs, but occasionally for other elements.

L521 Roof tiles and slates
1 Clay tiles
2 Concrete tiles
3 Fibre cement tiles
4 Slates
5 Natural stone roofing
Excludes natural slates.
6 Shingles

L522 Roof cladding sheets
1 Roof and wall cladding sheets
Wall cladding sheets see L5141.
2 Sarking

L523 Thatch

L524 Roof membranes
1 Built-up roof membranes
2 Single layer roof membranes

L525 Roof asphalt

L526 Roof screeds

L527 Roof finishing coatings
1 Solar reflective roof coatings

L529 Ancillary products for roof coverings, claddings, linings
1 Fixings
2 Slate and tile vents
3 Roof space vents
4 Edgings and trims
  1 Barge boards
  2 Soffit boards
  3 Eaves trims
  4 Flashings
  5 Verges

L53 Floor coverings, claddings, linings

Includes coverings mainly for floors, but occasionally for other elements.
For mosaics see L5121.

L531 Preformed flooring systems
Includes portable floors, convertible floors.
Gymnasium/dance flooring systems are at L84621.

L532 Strip flooring

L533 Tiles and blocks
1 Floor tiles
Includes heavy duty tiles.
  1 Promenade tiles
2 Floor blocks
Includes parquet.

L534 Pavings
1 Slabs, flags
2 Bricks
3 Setts, cobbles

L535 Floor screeds

L536 Floor covering sheets, flexible sheets
For ornamental carpets see L8711.
1 Carpet
  1 Underlay
2 Carpet tiles
3 Natural linoleum
4 Vinyl sheets, synthetic linoleum
5 Rubber sheets
9 Other

L537 Jointless flooring

L538 Floor finishing coatings
Floor paint is at L68245.
1 Floor seals

L539 Ancillary products for floor coverings, claddings, linings
1 Fixings
  1 Acoustic floor mountings
  2 Anti-vibration floor mountings
  3 Carpet grippers
  4 Stair rods
  5 Floor clips
2 Concrete floor treatments
  1 Curers
  2 Hardeners
  3 Seals

L54 Ceiling coverings, claddings

Includes coverings mainly for ceilings, but occasionally for other elements.

L541 Ceiling tiles

L542 Ceiling panels
Suspended ceilings are at L387.

L543 Ceiling finishing coatings
Plaster is at L551.

L549 Ancillary products for ceiling coverings, claddings, linings
1 Fixings

L55 General products for coverings and claddings

General purpose fixing/jointing products are at L67.
Fixings for wall coverings are at L5191.
Fixings for roof coverings are at L5291.
Fixings for floor coverings are at L5391.
Fixings for ceiling coverings are at L5491.
Formwork linings are at M2114.

L551 Plasters
1 Gypsum plasters
2 Lime plasters

L552 Levellings, linings

L553 Beddings, adhesives, grouts

L554 Movement/dividing joints, spacings

L555 Joint coverings
Flashings are at L52944.

L556 Mouldings, edgings, trims
1 Architraves
2 Arrises
3 Cornices, friezes
4 Coves
5 Ceiling roses
6 Pilasters
7 Scagliola
8 Dado rails/mouldings
9 Picture rails/mouldings

L557 Supports

L558 Reinforcements

L559 Other

L6 General purpose civil engineering and construction fabric products

---

L61 Loose granular fills, aggregates, chips

Fibres are at L633.

L611 Dense fills/aggregates
1 Blast furnace slag
2 Gravel
3 Sand
4 Crushed stone
5 Recycled brick/concrete
6 Iron ore
7 Barytes
8 Scrap iron

L612 Lightweight fills/aggregates
1 Clay, slate aggregates, expanded
2 Glass aggregate, expanded
3 Vermiculite
4 Perlite
5 Diatomaceous earth
6 Synthetic foam granules
7 Cork granules
8 Foamed/expanded slag
9 Sintered pulverised fuel ash

L613 Wood particles
Excludes cork.
1 Sawdust

L619 Other

L62 Binding agents

L621 Cement
1 Acid resistant cement
2 Rapid hardening cement

L622 Cement replacements
1 Natural pozzolan
2 Pulverised fuel ash
3 Microsilica
4 Ground granulated blast furnace slag

L623 Lime, hydraulic

L624 Lime, air hardening

L625 Bitumen, asphalt

L626 Resinous binders

L627 Gypsum

L63 Admixtures, additives

L631 Admixtures by type
- 01 Plasticizing agents
- 02 Water retaining agents
- 03 Water reducing agents
- 04 Air-entraining agents
- 05 Gas generating agents
- 06 Setting retarders
- 07 Setting accelerators
- 08 Frostproofing agents
- 09 Waterproofing agents
- 10 Oil proofing agents
- 11 Adherence proofing agents
- 12 Colouring agents
- 13 Admixtures for injections
- 14 Admixtures for projections
- 15 Expanding agents
- 16 Foaming agents

L632 Admixtures by use
- 1 Cement admixtures (general purpose)
- 2 Mortar admixtures

L633 Fibre reinforcement
- 1 Polymer
- 2 Glass
- 3 Steel
- 9 Other

L64 Mortars

Plasters are at L551.
Screeds are at L535.

L641 General purpose cement:sand mortar
- 1 Wet (ready to use)
- 2 Dry
- 3 Partial mix
  Requires addition of aggregate and water.

L642 Special purpose mortars
- 1 Epoxy mortars, other hydrocarbon mortars
- 2 Intumescent mortars

L65 General purpose sections

L651 Rigid sections
- 1 Timber sections
- 2 Steel sections
  L65121/3
  Hot-formed steel sections
  - 1 Open, flanged sections
  - 2 Circular hollow sections
  - 3 Rectangular hollow sections
  - 4 Cold-formed steel sections
- 3 Light-alloy sections
- 4 Plastic sections

L652 Flexible sections
- 1 Plastic sections
- 2 Rubber sections

L66 General purpose sheets

L661 Solid sheets

- 1 Fibre-silicate sheets

- 2 Plasterboard

- 3 Glass sheets
  - 01 Flat glass
    Includes float, plate, rolled, etc.
  - 02 Toughened glass
    Includes bullet resistant glass.
  - 03 Laminated glass
  - 04 Wired/corrugated wired glass
  - 05 Obscured/ translucent/ opaque glass
  - 06 Mirror glass
  - 07 Reflective/diffuse reflection glass
  - 08 Coloured/tinted glass
  - 09 Decorative glass
    Includes moulded glass panes, bullions.
  - 10 Solar control glass
  - 11 Safety glass
    Includes fire resistant glass.
  - 12 Double/multiple glazing
  - 13 Architectural glass
    - 1 Stained glass
    - 2 Engraved glass
    - 3 Other decorative finishes for glass
    - 4 Window leading materials

L661 *continued*

- 4 Steel sheets
  - 1 Flat
    - 1 Floor grating/checkerplate
    - 2 Hot rolled steel plate
  - 2 Profiled
    Includes structural profiled sheets for decking.
    Excludes profiled steel structural formwork – see L3321.

- 5 Aluminium/light-alloy sheets
  - 1 Flat
  - 2 Profiled

- 6 Other metal sheets

- 7 Plywood/blockboard/ laminboard
  - 1 Plain
  - 2 Veneered
  - 3 Polymer coated

- 8 Particle boards, firbreboards
  - 1 Hardboard
  - 2 Medium-density fibreboard (MDF)
  - 3 Insulating board
  - 4 Chipboard
  - 5 Oriented strand board (OSB)
  - 9 Other

- 9 Plastic sheets

L662 Hollow core sheets
- 1 Particle board, hollow core
- 2 Honeycomb sheets
- 3 Metal
- 4 Plastics

L663 Thin flexible sheets including textiles
- 1 Thin sheets, plastics
- 2 Thin sheets, metal
  - 1 Foils
- 3 Thin sheets, timber
  Includes veneers.
- 4 Textiles
- 5 Building papers
- 6 Rubber sheets
- 7 Mesh for general use
- 8 Lathing
  - 1 Angle beads
  - 2 Edging beads
  - 3 Arris protectors

L67 General purpose fixing/jointing products

Includes:
All general purpose fixings.
Examples: nails, screws, bolts, rivets, staples, plugs, etc.

Excludes:
Single purpose products such as structural fixings, fixings for coverings, fixings for proofings, etc. which are part of the specialised sections.
Architectural ironmongery is at L418.

L671 General purpose fixings

1 Products to accept fixings
  1 Plugs
  2 Anchor rails
  3 Anchor blocks
  4 Channels
  5 Sockets

2 Fixing products
  1 Threadless fixings
    1 Nails
    2 Panel pins
    3 Rivets
    4 Staples
  2 Threaded fixings
    1 Bolts and nuts
    2 Screws
  3 Chemical fixings
  4 Locating and locking devices
    e.g. dowels, clips, split pins.
  5 Adjusting fixings
    e.g. washers, cable adjusters.
  6 Bandings
  7 Cramps
  8 Anchors
    1 Anchor bolts
    2 Expanding bolts

L672 Welded joint products
1 Joint fillers for soldering
2 Joint fillers for brazing
3 Joint fillers for welding
  1 Joint fillers for electric welding
  2 Joint fillers for gas welding

L673 Adhesives
1 Natural adhesives/glues
2 Rubber-based adhesives
3 Two pack polymerising adhesives
  Includes epoxy resin adhesives.
9 Other

L674 General purpose tape
Includes masking tape.
Tape for services is at L7845.

L675 Joint fillers, sealants
1 Joint fillers
2 Putties
3 Glazing sealants
4 Construction sealants
5 Gaskets
  Includes glazing gaskets.

L676 Ropes, wires, cables
1 Ropes
2 Wires
3 Cables

L68 Proofings, insulation, paints, etc.

L681 Proofings, insulation
Classify here general proofing products for various uses in buildings and civil engineering works. Proofings for specific applications are classified with the relevant product; for example, climate control plant and services proofings are at L784.

1 Fireproofings
  Fireproofing for services is at L7842.
  Intumescent mortar is at L6422.
  1 Boards etc.
  2 Blankets, quilts, rolls, etc.
  3 Casings
    Includes pre-formed and lined steel sheet.
  4 Fire seals/stops
    Excludes those for services.
  5 Flame retardant coatings/paints
  6 Intumescent coatings/paints
  7 Sprayed coatings

2 Dampproofings
  Includes condensation control.
  1 Membranes
  2 Coatings
  3 Chemical injection
  4 Vapour barriers

3 Waterproofing
  Classify here waterproofing products which are for application to many different building/civil engineering elements.
  Specialist products for below ground waterproofing (tanking) are at L6814.
  Specialist products for roof waterproofing are at L522 and L525.
  1 Boards etc.
  2 Membranes
    Includes liquid membranes.
  3 Coatings

4 Tanking
  1 Tiles, panels, etc.
  2 Coatings

5 Thermal insulation
  1 Panels, slabs, boards, etc.
  2 Quilts, rolls, etc.
  3 Preformed casings
  4 Coatings
  5 Sprayed coatings
  6 Loose fill

L681 *continued*

6 Acoustic insulation
  1 Panels, slabs, etc.
  2 Quilts, rolls, etc.
  3 Coatings

7 Vibration insulation
  Includes structural bearings.
  Vibration damping for HVAC is at L7843.
  Anti-vibration floor mountings are at L53912.
  1 Pads

8 Prevention of biological/chemical attack/damage
  1 Coatings to prevent biological attack
  2 Coatings to prevent chemical damage

9 Prevention of abrasive wear
  1 Coatings

L682 Paints and varnishes
1 Primers, undercoats
2 General purpose finishing coats
  1 Solvent based
  2 Water based
3 Textured paints
4 Specialised function paints
  Fireproofing paints are at L681156.
  1 Solar reflective paints
  2 Fluorescent paints
  3 Corrosion prevention paints
    Corrosion prevention coatings are at L685.
  4 Line paints for sports grounds
    Line markers are at L81316.
  5 Floor paints
  6 Masonry paints
  7 Road marking paints
5 Varnishes

L683 Surface impregnation products
1 Decorative surface impregnations
  e.g. stains.
  1 Decorative timber conservation products
2 Protective surface impregnations
  Includes immersion treatments.
  1 Surface consolidation/hardening impregnations
  2 Dirt inhibiting impregnations
  3 Impregnations protecting from biological attack, timber preservatives
  4 Impregnations preventing static electricity
  5 Water repellent impregnations
  6 Non-skid proofings
  7 Anti-graffiti impregnations

L684 Other surface forming products
1 Glazes
2 Gilding
3 Lacquers
4 Vitreous enamelling

L685 **Corrosion prevention coatings**
*Corrosion prevention paints
are at L68243.*
1 Galvanised coatings
2 Anodised coatings
3 Electro-plated coatings
4 Stoved organic finishes
e.g. polyester powder coatings.

L686 **Vermin control**
1 Insect control
2 Bird control
3 Rodent control

L69 **General cleaning products**

L691 **Detergents**

L692 **Solvents**

L693 **Spot removing products**

L694 **Graffiti removing products**

L695 **Paint strippers**

L696 **Polish**

L7   Services

L71 **Supply/storage/distribution of liquids and gases**

L711 **Water and general supply/storage/distribution**
Classify here general products which may be used for the supply/storage/distribution of water, steam, gas or special liquids.

1 Complete supply and distribution sets for water supply
  1 Packaged plumbing units

2 Cold water storage
  Classify here general storage products.
  1 Rainwater tanks
  2 Supply water tanks
    1 Cisterns
    2 Cylinders
      For storage cylinders as part of a heating system, use L711351.

3 Hot water storage
  Includes self contained storage/heating units for hot water supply.
  Boilers for central heating/hot water supply are at L7521.
  1 Storage water heaters
  2 Immersion water heaters
  3 Calorifiers
  4 Instantaneous water heaters
  5 Ancillary products
    1 Hot water cylinders
    2 Cylinder jackets

4 Pumps for water supply/distribution
  Classify here general pumps for liquid/gas supply.
  Circulation pumps for HVAC systems are at L7531.
  Pumps for wet waste disposal (small scale) are at L7316.
  Pressure boosting pumps for showers are at L72107.
  1 Pump sets (combined booster pumps and pressurised vessels)
  2 Booster pumps
  3 Pressurised vessels
  4 Submersible pumps
    e.g. for fountains.
  5 Swimming pool pumps
  9 Other pumps

L711 *continued*

5 Water treatment
  Includes products for local/domestic use.
  Municipal water treatment products are at L21711.
  1 Water filters, purifiers
    Includes sterilisers, cleaners.
  2 Water softeners, conditioners
    Includes limescale inhibitors, removers.
  3 Ionizers, ozone treatment
  4 Additives for water treatment
  5 Swimming pool water treatment
  6 Ornamental pool water treatment

6 Pipes and pipework for water supply/distribution
  Classify here general pipework products for liquid/gas supply/distribution.
  Pipes for wet waste disposal are at L731 (small scale) and L21721 (sewers).
  HVAC ducts are at L7561.
  Mains pipes for water supply are at L217121.
  Pipework and ductwork ancillaries are at L781.
  1 Complete sets
  2 Supply pipes
  3 Pipe couplings/connectors
  4 Expansion joints
  5 Vibration (hammer) arrestors
  6 Pressure reducers

7 Valves for water supply/distribution
  Classify here general valves for liquid/gas supply/distribution.
  HVAC ductwork valves are at L75611.
  Includes water services valves at customers' boundaries.
  1 Boundary chambers/stopcock chambers
  2 Inlet/outlet valves
  3 Isolation valves
  4 Adjusting valves
  5 Controlling valves
  6 Non-return valves
  7 Mixing valves
  8 Stopcocks

8 Water meters

L712 **Steam supply/storage/distribution**
1 Complete supply and distribution sets for steam supply
2 Components of steam supply systems

L713 Gas supply/storage/distribution
For supply/storage of liquidised fuel gas see L714.
1 Complete supply and distribution sets for gases
2 Storage of gases
  1 Vacuum/pressurised air supply
  2 Vessels for medical gases
  3 Tanks for chemical/toxic gases
3 Compressors/pumps for gas supply/distribution
Compressors/fans for HVAC are at L753.
  1 Gas compressors
  2 Vacuum pumps
  3 Pumps for industrial/medical gases
4 Treatment for industrial/medical gases
5 Gas meters
6 Terminals for supplied gases
General taps are at L7251.
  1 Gas taps

L714 Liquid fuel supply/storage/distribution
Includes liquidised fuel gas.
1 Liquid fuel storage, tanks (atmospheric pressure)
2 Storage vessels, fuel gas and LPG (pressurised)
3 Liquid fuel pumps

L715 Supply, storage and distribution of special liquids
1 Complete supply and distribution sets for special liquids
Includes chemical/toxic and industrial/medical liquids.
2 Storage for special liquids
3 Pumps for special liquids
4 Treatment for special liquids

L716 Fixed fire suppression systems
1 Complete fixed fire suppression sets
2 Gaseous fire suppression
3 Chemical and foam fire suppression
4 Water mist (fine water spray)
5 Fire sprinklers
6 Deluge suppression
7 Fire suppression components
Portable fire extinguishers, hose reels are at L88.
  1 Fire hydrants
  2 Fire fighting media (foam, powder)
  3 Fire pumps
  4 Sprinkler heads

L72 Sanitary, laundry, cleaning equipment

L721 Sanitary equipment
Includes bathroom suites.
01 Baths
  1 Spa baths, whirlpool baths
  2 Deep soaking tubs
  3 Sitzbaths
  4 Baths with steps and/or seating
02 Bath panels
03 Splashbacks
04 Washbasins
  1 Vanity units
  2 Hairdressers' basins
  3 Cloakroom hand rinse basins
05 Drinking fountains
06 Washing fountains, troughs
07 Showers
Includes emergency showers, water heaters for showers.
08 Shower cabinets
09 Bath/shower screens, curtains
10 Shower trays
11 Toilets
  1 Biological toilets
  2 Chemical toilets
  3 Pans, seats
  4 WC cisterns
  5 Connectors
12 Bidets
13 Urinals
  1 Trough urinals
  2 Slab urinals
  3 Stall urinals
  4 Bowl urinals
  5 Sparge pipes
14 Sanitary disposal units
15 Sanitary macerators/crushers
Combined macerator-pumps are at L73161.
16 Sanitary incinerators
Other local solid waste incinerators are at L73231.
17 Sauna equipment
18 Footbaths
19 Communal washing units

L722 Laundry equipment
1 Washing machines
2 Clothes driers
3 Clothes airers
4 Trouser presses
5 Ironing/pressing equipment
6 Laundry folding machines
7 Laundry sinks, troughs
8 Clothes lines
  1 Rotary lines
  2 Retractable lines
9 Dry cleaning equipment

L723 Other fittings linked to water supply and removal systems
1 Dishwashers
2 Sinks for kitchens, bars
3 Equipment for laboratories, medical use, etc.
  1 Sinks, troughs
  2 Bedpan washers
  3 Surgical instrument sterilising equipment
4 Draining boards
5 Icemakers
6 Waste disposal units

L724 Cleaning equipment
1 Room cleaning equipment
  1 Vacuum cleaners
  2 Polishing machines
  3 Carpet cleaning equipment
  9 Others
2 High pressure washing equipment

L725 Ancillary sanitary, laundry, cleaning equipment
1 Taps/terminals for water supply
Classify here general taps for liquid/gas supply/distribution.
  1 Taps
    1 Mixer taps
    2 Spray taps
    3 Bibcocks
2 Plugs and chains
3 Overflow fittings

L73 Waste handling equipment

L731 Wet waste handling products
Pipes for water supply/distribution are at L7116.
1 Complete wet waste handling systems
2 Underground pipes and fittings
Includes pipes and fittings which connect a building or other works to a mains system. Mains pipes and sewers are at L217.
3 Sanitary above ground pipes and fittings
  1 Valves for sanitary pipes and fittings
4 Rainwater pipes and fittings
Rainwater tanks are at L71121.
  1 Complete pipe/guttering systems
  2 Fascia/guttering systems
  3 Internal rainwater systems
  4 Roof outlets
  5 Gutters
  6 Downpipes/drain pipes
  7 Siphonic drains
5 Channels, gullies and gratings
Channels, gullies and gratings for road/runway drainage are at L2123.

L731 *continued*

6 Local wet waste pumps
  1 Combined macerator-pumps
    Sanitary macerator/crushers
    are at L72115.
7 Local wet waste treatment
  Large scale sewage treatment
  products are at L2173.
  1 Package plant
  2 Septic tanks
  3 Cesspools
8 Alarm systems for liquids

L732 Solid waste handling products
1 Complete solid waste
  handling systems
2 Local solid waste collection
  1 Hoppers
  2 Refuse disposal chutes
  3 Dust control equipment
3 Local solid waste treatment
  Refuse disposal plant is at
  L2174.
  1 Incinerators
    Sanitary incinerators are at
    L72116.
  2 Compactors and balers
  3 Crushers
  4 Shredding machines

**L733 Gaseous waste handling
products**
Extractor units are at L7534.
1 Complete gaseous waste
  handling systems
2 Flues and chimneys
  Industrial chimneys are at
  L2181.
  1 Complete flue and chimney
    systems
  2 Flue linings
  3 Flue terminals, chimney pots
    Includes caps and cowls.
  4 Flue gas/fume treatment
    devices
  5 Flue accessories
3 Alarm systems for gases

L74	Electric power and lighting services products

*Devices to produce, supply,
distribute and use electrical
energy.*

Includes:
*All services products to produce,
supply and distribute electrical
power to and within the building;
luminaires, lamps and illuminated
indoor and outdoor signs.*

Excludes:
*Heaters – see section L752;
fans and air treatment units – see
sections L753/L754;
automatic signal devices such as
traffic lights – see section L2151.*

L741 Power storage devices
1 Batteries
  *Includes standby and
  emergency batteries.*
2 Uninterruptible power supply
  (UPS)
3 Other power storage devices

L742 Transformation devices
1 Electrical generators
  Includes emergency generators.
  1 Electrical generating sets
  2 Turbine driven generating
    sets
  3 Engine driven generating sets
    (gas or liquid fuel)
  4 Wind driven generating sets
  5 Combined electrical motor
    and generating sets
  6 Photovoltaic cells/solar panels
2 Transformers/converters
  1 Transformers
  2 Conversion sets
3 Electric motors
  1 Direct current motors
  2 Alternating current motors

L743 Protection devices
1 Devices to protect against
  electric shocks
2 Protection of electricity supply
  1 Devices to protect against
    excess current (fuses, circuit
    breakers)
  2 Overvoltage arresters
  3 Fault protection devices
3 Lightning conductors

L744 Treatment devices
1 Power factor control devices
2 Harmonic control devices

**L745 Measuring and recording
devices**
1 Meters
  1 Power meters
  2 Voltage meters
  3 Resistance meters
  4 Frequency meters
  5 Multi-meters
2 Recording devices
  1 Watt-hour recorders
    (electricity meters)

L746 Distribution devices
1 Power supply control devices
  1 Switches
    Light switches are at L74735.
  2 Distribution boards
  3 Photoelectric cells
2 Conductors
  1 LV cables
    1 Wiring cables
  2 HV cables
  3 Busbars
3 Conduit, trunking and ducts
  (floor ducting, cable
  protection)
  *Ductwork for HVAC is at L7561.
  General trunking is at L7822.*
4 Control gear (switchgear,
  relays, etc.)
5 Conductor couplings
6 Junction boxes, terminal
  boxes
7 Insulators/insulation (other
  than cable protection)

L747 Terminal devices

1 Socket outlets
  1 Shaving sockets
  2 Adapters
  3 Socket protectors

2 Plug connectors (pin plugs)

3 Fixed luminaires (lighting
  fittings)
  *Includes luminaires for internal
  and/or external use.*
  1 Fixed luminaires for general
    lighting
    *Includes chandeliers,
    uplighters, downlighters, etc.*
  2 Circulation luminaires
    1 Emergency lighting
    2 Illuminated signs
      Road signs are at L2152.
    3 Navigation lighting
  3 Specialised location
    luminaires
    1 Medical/hospital lighting
    2 Display lighting
    3 Stage, theatre, nightclub
      lighting
    4 TV/film studio lighting
    5 Photographic lighting
    6 Underwater lighting
    7 Street lighting
      *Lighting columns are at
      L81102.*
    8 Lasers
  4 Special purpose luminaires
    1 Impact resistant lighting
      *Includes anti-vandal
      lighting.*
    2 Flameproof lighting
    3 Dustproof lighting
    4 Non-corroding lighting
    5 Waterproof lighting
      *Underwater lighting is at
      L747336.*
    6 Infra-red lighting
    7 Ultra-violet lighting
    8 Floodlighting

L747 3 continued

5 Light switches
1 Dimmer switches
2 Dolly/rocker switches
3 Switches for flashing light effects
4 Light-sensitive switches
5 Lighting time switches
6 Lighting accessories
1 Diffusers
2 Lampholders
3 Lighting track
4 Ballasts for fluorescent lamps
5 Lampshades

4 Lamps
1 Light bulbs (incandescent lamps)
2 Halogen lamps
3 Discharge lamps
   Includes fluorescent lamps, neon lamps, etc.
4 Fibre optic lamps

5 Lighting sources other than electricity
   Includes gas (mains and bottled), paraffin, oil.

L75 Climate control plant and equipment (HVAC)

L751 Complete climate control systems
Local cooling/air conditioning units are at L7526.
1 Complete heating systems
   1 Micro-CHP packages
2 Complete cooling systems
3 Complete mechanical ventilation systems
   (without air treatment)
4 Complete air conditioning systems
   1 Purpose designed central air conditioning systems
   2 Packaged systems, self-contained
   3 Packaged systems, split system
      Includes systems with separate air handling and condensing units.
   4 Close control systems
      e.g. for computer rooms.

L752 Transformation and conversion of energy

L7521/4
Heat production
Includes central heating systems.

....

1 Boilers, central heat generators
   Boilers here are central heat generators which produce hot water for heating systems (and also often for hot water supply). For heat generators solely for hot water supply see L7113.
   1 Gas fired boilers
   2 Oil fired boilers
   3 Electric boilers
   4 Solid fuel boilers
   5 Multi-fuel boilers
   6 Heat generators, warm air
   7 Steam generators
   8 Heat generators, thermal liquid

2 Electric heaters
   Electrically heated towel rails are at L75626.
   1 Convectors
      Includes fan convectors.
   2 Storage heaters
   3 Combined convector/convector-storage heaters
   4 Electric bar heaters (electric fires)
   5 Radiant heat and light
   6 Halogen heat lamps
   9 Other electric heaters
      1 Embedded electric heating terminals
         Includes underfloor, wall and ceiling heating.
      2 Surface heating products

3 Non-electric local heating units
   1 Gas fires
   2 Space heaters (other than electric)
      Includes commercial/industrial space heaters.
   3 Open fires (solid fuel)
   4 Stoves (solid fuel)
   5 Oil heaters
   6 Fires with back boilers

4 Heat pumps

....

5 Refrigeration/freeze plant
   1 Refrigerant condensers
   2 Refrigerant evaporators
   3 Refrigerant compressors
   4 Refrigerant coolers
   5 Refrigeration and freeze media

6 Local cooling/air conditioning units
   1 Room air conditioners, self-contained
   2 Portable air conditioning units
   3 Air curtains

L752 continued

7 Solar collectors

8 Heat exchangers

9 Cooling towers
   Small scale, as part of HVAC systems.
   For large scale cooling towers see L21821.

L753 Impelling equipment
Supply pumps are at L7114.
Supply compressors are at L7133.
1 HVAC circulation pumps
   1 Circulation pumps, hot water
   2 Circulation pumps, chilled water
   3 Pumps accessories
2 HVAC compressors
3 HVAC fans for ductlines
4 Mechanical ventilation, extraction
   Other gaseous waste handling products are at L733.
   1 Industrial extraction fans
   2 Emergency smoke/fire extraction/vents
      Includes smoke curtains.
   3 Fume cupboards, fume extraction
   4 Fans, domestic
      Includes extract fans for kitchen/bathroom use.
   5 Fan accessories
   6 Room air circulation fans
5 Natural ventilation/extraction
   1 Passive stack ventilation systems
   2 Wind tower ventilation systems

L754 Treatment
1 Treatment of circulation liquids
2 Supply air treatment
   1 Air filters
   2 Humidifiers
   3 Dehumidifiers
   4 Ionizers
   5 Air fresheners

L755 Measuring, detection and control devices
1 Temperature controls
   1 Zone controls
   2 Optimum start controls
   3 Programmers
   4 Room thermostats
   5 Frost-stats
2 Plant and services control
   1 Pressure controls
   2 Flow controls
   3 Concentration controls

L756   **Distribution**
Distribution pipes for water are at L7116.
1 Ductwork, ducts
   Ancillary ductwork products are at L781.
   Electrical ductwork is at L7463.
  1 Ductwork valves
  2 Fire dampers for air ductlines
  3 Fire shutters for air ductlines
  4 Guide vanes
  5 Air mixers
  6 Ductwork couplings/
     connectors
  7 Access fittings for ductwork
  8 Duct silencers
2 Central heating terminals
   i.e. devices which emit heat supplied by a remote source, but do not generate heat themselves.
  1 Radiators
    1 Air separators
    2 Radiator valves
      Includes thermostatic valves.
  2 Convectors for central heating
  3 Radiation panels
  4 Embedded heating terminals
  5 Finned pipes
  6 Heated towel rails
    Other towel rails are at L8245.
  9 Other heating terminals
3 Terminals for treated/
   untreated air
   Includes grilles, louvres, diffusers, etc.

L757   **Maintenance and testing products**
1 Maintenance of climate control and services plant
2 Plant and service test equipment

| **L76** | **Information/communication services products** |

Includes:
Individual and centralised systems and devices for sound, image and data interception or receiving, transmission and emission, incorporated in a permanent way in the construction. Includes building automation and management systems, automatic signalling systems in buildings, automatic traffic signalling systems.

Excludes:
Information boards, signs (illuminated signs).

L761   **General information systems**
Provided to anyone within range of the delivery device, without two-way transmission.
1 Audio information
  1 Audio systems
  2 Sound signal systems
  3 Public address systems
  4 Paging systems
  5 Amplifiers
  6 Loudspeakers
  7 Microphones
  8 Induction loop systems
2 Visual information
   Visual message systems are at L8459.
  1 Time distribution systems
  2 News tray systems
  3 Projection systems
    1 Projection screens
    2 Slide projectors
    3 Overhead projectors
  4 Visual signals for buildings
3 Audio-visual information
   Includes multi-media.
  1 Broadcasting equipment
  2 Broadcast receiving equipment
    Includes television aerials, satellite dishes.
  3 AV recording equipment
  4 Presentation systems
    1 Video monitors/walls
    2 Film projectors

L762   **Safety and security information systems**
1 Access controls
  1 Access and counting systems
  2 Code reading systems
  3 Electronic key systems
2 Presence detection
  01 Intruder alarms
    Includes automatic 999 dialling and direct line to central control point systems.
  02 Surveillance mirrors
  03 Micro-switch contacts for doors and windows
  04 Pressure mats
  05 Continuous wiring systems
  06 Vibration detector systems
  07 Light beam systems
    Includes laser systems.
  08 Infra-red radiation detectors
  09 Microphone connected noise detectors
  10 Ultrasonic systems
  11 Microwave detectors
  12 Air pressure differential systems
  13 Electrical capacitance systems
  14 Manual alert control
3 Emergency alarms
  1 Alarm systems for the disabled
4 Built-in failure detection
5 Fire/smoke detection/alarm systems
  1 Complete fire detection/alarm systems
  2 Control and indicating equipment
  3 Fire/smoke detectors
  4 Alarms/sounders
  5 Alarm glass
6 Closed circuit television systems (CCTV)
   CCTV systems for pipe inspection are at L766.
  1 Cameras
  2 Monitors
7 Door bells/chimes

L763   **Communication systems (two-way transmission)**
1 Telephone based systems
  1 Single line telephone systems
    1 Answering machines
    2 Fax machines
  2 Multiple line telephone systems
    1 Private automatic branch exchange systems (PABX)
    2 Direct in-dialling systems (DID)
2 Intercom systems
  1 Door entry telephones
3 Conference systems

L764   **Building management systems**
Includes integrated comfort and safety controls.

L765 Pipe inspection CCTV systems

L766 Communication cables
1 Coaxial
2 Fibre optic
3 Other

L77 Transport services products

L771 Lifts
1 Suspended
2 Hydraulic
3 Rack and pinion
4 Scissor lifts
5 Stairlifts
6 Hoists for disabled users

L772 Escalators, conveyors
1 Moving pavements, travellators
2 Escalators
3 Goods conveyors

L773 Building envelope maintenance systems
1 Platforms, cradles
2 Hoists
3 Roof trolley systems
4 Gantries
5 Safety tracks, cradle tracks

L774 Tube conveyors
e.g. document conveying.

L775 Automated guided systems
1 Automated document filing and retrieval
2 Automated guided vehicles

L78 General purpose and ancillary services products

L781 Ancillary pipework and ductwork products
1 Sealants for services
2 Network identification
  1 Identification tape
3 Pipe/duct collars
4 Pipe/duct closures
5 Pipe/duct supports
  1 Clamps
  2 Shoes
  3 Slide bearings
  4 Plates
  5 Test plugs

L782 Services supports and enclosures
HVAC ducting is at L7561.
1 Conduit and fittings
2 Trunking
  Electrical trunking is at L7463.
  1 Skirting/dado trunking systems
  2 Underfloor trunking
3 Cable trays/ladders
4 Underground enclosures

L783 General fixings for services
1 Cable clips
2 Magnetic fixings

L784 Proofings/insulation/tape for services
1 Thermal insulation and linings
  1 Pipe lagging
2 Fire proofing
  1 Pipe sleeves
  2 Pipe pillows
3 Vibration damping
4 Acoustic insulation
5 Tape
  General purpose tape is at L674.
  1 Frost protection tapes
  2 Corrosion resistant tapes
  3 Jointing tape
    Includes PTFE tape.

L785 Products for maintenance of services
CCTV systems for pipe inspection see L766.
1 Pipe/drain clearing/unblocking
2 Leak repair for pipework
3 Descaling products
4 Lubricants

L786 Measuring, detection and control devices
1 General measuring instruments
  1 Thermometers
  2 Concentration measuring
  3 Volume measuring
  4 Level measuring
  5 Weighing instruments
  6 Moisture detectors, meters
2 Plant and service controls
  1 Leak detection
  2 Cable monitoring
3 Hydraulic and pneumatic process controls

L8 Fixtures and furnishings

L81 External furniture and fittings

L811 Street furniture
01 Bollards
  1 Collapsible bollards (for parking)
  2 Illuminated bollards
02 Public lighting columns
03 Bicycle racks
04 Seating and tables for public external use
05 Litter bins
06 Storage fittings for services and maintenance
07 Flagpoles
08 Weathervanes
09 Memorials, statuary
10 Salt/grit bins
11 Advertising hoardings
  Poster display units are at L8455.
12 Pedestrian signs, finger posts
13 Bus shelters
14 Tree grilles
  1 Tree guards, ties
15 Street nameplates

L812 Garden and park furniture
01 Garden/patio seating and tables
02 Garden umbrellas
03 Bird baths
04 Bird boxes
05 Tubs for plants
06 Sundials
07 Garden ornaments
08 Horticultural products
09 Vegetable plants
10 Plant protection devices
11 External pools, ponds, lakes
  Includes linings.
12 Ornamental fountains

L813 Playground, sports ground fittings, equipment
1 Sports grounds and fittings
  1 Grass/turf
    (for playing fields, football pitches, etc.)
  2 Artificial grass/turf
  3 Other porous surfaces
    Includes all-weather tracks for athletics, cycling, etc.
  4 Artificial ski slopes
  5 Artificial ice rinks
  6 Line markers
    Line paints are at L68244.
  7 Goalposts etc.

L813   *continued*

  2 Playground fittings
    1 Climbing frames
    2 Slides
    3 Swings
    4 Roundabouts
    5 Animals, springers
    6 Special needs playground
      fittings
    7 Safety surfaces
      Includes tan bark, sand, grit,
      etc.
  3 Swimming pools
    1 Water slides, flumes
    2 Diving boards
    3 Ladders

L82   Domestic and general furniture
         and fittings

L821   Cloakroom and clothes storage
         furniture, fittings
  01 Wardrobes
  02 Chests of drawers
  03 Lockers
  04 Coat racks
  05 Hatstands
  06 Shoe trees
  07 Coat hooks
  08 Coat hangers
  09 Cloakroom units
  10 Umbrella stands
  11 Clothes drying cabinets
  12 Wardrobe rails

L822   Living and dining room furniture
  1 Tables
    Includes coffee tables, dining
    tables, etc.
  2 Chairs
    Chairs for restaurants and
    canteens are at L8342.
    Chairs for offices are at L8533.
  3 Settees, easy chairs
  4 Stools
  5 Benches
  6 Chaises longues
  7 Sofa beds, chair beds, futons

L823   Bedroom furniture
  1 Beds
    Hospital beds are at L8522.
    1 Foldaway beds
    2 Bunk beds
    3 Divans
    4 Waterbeds
  2 Headboards
  3 Cots, cradles
  4 Bedside units
  5 Dressing tables
  6 Nursery/children's furniture
  7 Mattresses

L824   Bathroom, toilet furniture and
         fittings
         Sanitary bathroom equipment is at
         L721.
  1 Bathroom cabinets
  2 Driers
    1 Hand driers
    2 Face driers
    3 Hair driers
    4 Whole body driers
  3 Towel dispensers
  4 Sanitary dispensers
  5 Towel rails
    Heated towel rails are at
    L75626.
  6 Soap holders/dispensers
  7 Nappy changing units

L825   Non-clothes storage furniture
  01 Cupboards
  02 Chests
  03 Sideboards
  04 Dressers
  05 Filing cabinets
  06 Plan/map chests
  07 Desk tidies
  08 Meter cabinets
  09 Movable aisle systems
  10 Carousels
    1 Vertical carousels
    2 Horizontal carousels
  11 Trolleys
  12 Computer print-out storage
  13 Computer tape/disk storage
  14 Microfilm/fiche storage
  15 Index storage systems
  16 Rotary storage systems
  17 Suspension storage
     systems
  18 Fire resistant storage

L826   Shelving
         Library shelving is at L8431.
  1 Shelves
  2 Supports, brackets
  3 Racking

L827   Refuse disposal furniture
  1 Bins
  2 Ashtrays
  3 Refuse bag holders
  4 Sanitary waste disposal
    containers

L828   Fireplaces
         Flues are at L7332.
  1 Fire surrounds
  2 Firebacks
  3 Fenders
  4 Hearths
  5 Hoods

L829   Garage furniture, fittings

L83   Catering furniture

L831   Kitchen furniture
  1 Complete sets
  2 Single units
    1 Floor units
    2 Wall units
  3 Kitchen worktops
  4 Kitchenettes

L832   Specialised food storage and
         display furniture
  1 Refrigerators
  2 Freezers
  3 Fridge-freezers
  4 Hot cupboards
  5 Cold cabinets, refrigerated
    display cabinets
    1 Drinks chillers
    2 Water coolers
  6 Bottle racks
  7 Bains marie
  8 Snack cabinets

L833   Food preparing and serving
         furniture
  1 Catering ventilation
    1 Extractor hoods
  2 Cookers, ovens, stoves
  3 Hotplates
  4 Ranges
  5 Grills
  6 Fryers
  7 Barbecues
  8 Small specialised cooking
    equipment
  9 Drink making equipment

L834   Restaurant, canteen furniture
  1 Bars and serveries
    Bar sinks are at L7232.
    1 Refrigerated bars
  2 Chairs, seating units
    Chairs for living/dining rooms
    are at L8222.
    Chairs for offices are at L8533.
  3 Tables

L84   Educational, cultural, display
         furniture, fittings

L841   Educational, entertainment
         furniture, fittings
         Includes schools, theatres,
         concert halls, cinemas, stadia.
  1 Auditorium seating
  2 Classroom furniture
  3 Stages
  4 Podia
  5 Spectator stands
  6 Scenery docks
  7 Suspension systems
  8 Curtain sets

L842 Religious furniture, fittings
01 Religious seating, pews
02 Lecterns
03 Pulpits
04 Choir screens
05 Organs, organ cases/ screens
06 Fonts
07 Synagogue furniture
08 Mosque furniture
09 Temple furniture
10 Funerary furniture and fittings
11 Crematoria furniture and fittings
12 Bells, bellframes, fittings

L843 Library and archive furniture, fittings
1 Shelving
   General shelving is at L826.
2 Filing furniture
3 Display furniture

L844 Museum, art gallery furniture, fittings
1 Display cabinets, racks
2 Gallery hanging systems
3 Stands, pedestals
4 Museum showcases

L845 General display furniture, fittings
1 Exhibition stands, shell schemes
2 Display screens
3 Pin boards, notice boards
4 Writing boards
   1 Blackboards
   2 Dry marker boards
5 Poster display units
   Advertising hoardings are at L81111.
   1 Illuminated
   2 Indoor
   3 Outdoor
6 Information signs
   1 Nameplates
7 Lettering and numerals
8 Plaques
9 Visual message systems
   1 Scoreboards
   2 Moving light displays
   3 Indicator boards

L846 Sports, leisure fittings, equipment
1 Arcade machines
2 Gymnasium equipment
   1 Gymnasium/dance flooring systems
   Floor coverings and claddings are at L53.
3 Fitness and exercise equipment
4 Nets
5 Equipment storage racks

L85 Work environment furniture, fittings

L851 Scientific furniture, fitments
Laboratory sinks are at L72331; fume cupboards are at L75343.
1 Laboratory furniture, workbenches, etc.
2 Laboratory worktops
3 Language laboratory equipment
4 Sterilisation and contamination control equipment

L852 Medical furniture, fittings
1 Consulting couches
2 Hospital beds
3 Hospital bedheads
4 Curtains/screening
5 Medical equipment stands
6 Operating theatre equipment
7 Mortuary furniture, fittings
8 Post-mortem/dissection tables
9 Dentistry fittings

L853 Office furniture
1 Desks
   1 Reception desks
   2 Computer desks
2 Drawing office equipment, drawing boards
3 Seating, office chairs
   Chairs for living/dining rooms are at L8222.
   Chairs for restaurants/canteens are at L8342.
4 Ergonomic computer accessories
   1 Footrests
   2 Armrests
   3 Copyholders

L854 Manufacturing furniture
1 Workbenches
2 Darkroom fittings
   Sinks and troughs for dark-room use are at L72331.

L855 Agricultural furniture, fittings

L856 Abattoir fittings

L857 Shop furniture, vending machines
Food storage and display furniture is at L832.
1 Counters
2 Shop display fittings
   1 Mobile display fittings
3 Shop storage fittings
4 Vending machines
   1 Packaged goods vending machines
   2 Food and drink vending machines
   Includes ice cream vending machines.
   3 Sanitary product vending machines
   4 Contraceptives vending machines
   5 Printed products vending machines
5 Ticket machines
6 Change machines
7 Specialised retail shelving

L858 Security furniture
1 Bank/building society fittings
   1 Anti-bandit screens
   2 Automated banking equipment
   3 Counters
2 Safes, strongrooms, vaults
3 Point of sale units/tills
4 Key security cabinets
5 Prison furniture and fittings

L86 Communication fittings

L861 Post boxes

L862 Postroom racks

L863 Pigeonholes

L864 Post trolleys

L865 Post handling equipment

L866 Telephone booths

L867 Acoustic hoods

L868 Directory boards

L87   Furnishings, ornaments, internal decoration

L89   Furniture accessories

L871   Soft furnishings
1 Rugs/ornamental carpets
Carpets are at L5361.
2 Mats
3 Mat frames
4 Curtains, drapes
Includes sun curtaining.
Shower curtains are at L72109.
Hospital curtains/screening are at L8524.
Blinds are at L422.
　1 Curtain tracks, rods, fittings
　2 Pelmets, swags, tie-backs
5 Upholstery
6 Cushions, padding, beanbags
7 Bedding
8 Tablecloths, placemats, etc.
9 Trimmings

L872   Plant display furniture
1 Planters
2 Vases
3 Indoor plants
　1 Flowers
　2 Irrigation systems
4 Artificial plants

L873   Ornaments, decoration
1 Ornaments
Includes pottery, ceramics, carvings, etc.
2 Mirrors
3 Ornamental screens
4 Artworks
Includes paintings, prints, sculpture, photographs, murals, etc.
5 Clocks
6 Wallhangings
　1 Tapestries

L874   Internal pools, ponds
Includes linings.

L891   Cabinet hardware
1 Drawer slides/runners
2 Castors
3 Locks for furniture
4 Flapstays

L88   Portable fire suppression systems

L881   Fire extinguishers

L882   Hoses, hose reels and enclosures/cabinets
1 Fire hoses
2 Fire hose reels
3 Fire hose enclosures/cabinets

L883   Fire blankets

L884   Fire buckets

A

Abattoir fittings L856
Abrasive wear prevention
   products L6819
Access control systems L7621
Access fittings for ductwork L75617
Access floors L386
Access ladders L43211
Access products L41
Acid resistant cement L6211
Acoustic doors L41124
Acoustic floor mountings L53911
Acoustic hoods L867
Acoustic insulation L6816
   for services L7844
Adapters L74712
Additives
   cement/mortar L63
   local water treatment L71154
Adherence proofing agents
   (admixtures) L63111
Adhesives L673
   for coverings/claddings L553
Adjusting fixings L67125
Adjusting valves L71174
Admixtures L63
   mortar L6322
Admixtures for cement and
   mortar L6321
Advertising hoardings L81111
Aerated concrete blocks L32232
Aerials L76132
Aggregates L61
   dense L611
   lightweight L612
Agricultural furniture/fittings L855
Air bricks L3274
Air conditioning systems
   complete L7514
Air conditioning units (local) L7526
Air curtains L75263
Air filters L75421
Air fresheners L75425
Air mixers L75615
Air pressure differential alarm
   systems L762212
Air separators for radiators L756211
Air transport products L212
Air-entraining agents
   (admixtures) L63104
Airers for clothes L7223
Alarm glass L76255
Alarm systems
   fire/smoke L7625
   for the disabled L76231
   gases L7333
   liquids L7318
   security L7622
All-weather tracks for athletics/
   cycling L81313
Alternating current motors L74232
Aluminium sheets L6615
Amplifiers L76115
Anchor blocks L67113
Anchor bolts L671281
Anchor heads L1151
Anchor rails L67112
Anchor tendons L1152
Anchorages
   ground L11
   prestressing L3347
Anchors L67128
   ground L11
Angle beads L66381
Angle hinges L418307

Animal models for
   playgrounds L81325
Anodised coatings L6852
Answering machines L763111
Anti skid texturing L21106
Anti-bandit screens L85811
Anti-corrosion treatments/coatings
   coatings L685
   paints L68243
Anti-graffiti impregnations L68327
Anti-intruder barriers L443
Anti-vandal lighting L747341
Anti-vibration floor mountings L53912
Approach indicators L21582
Arcade machines L8461
Architectural glass L661313
Architectural ironmongery L418
Architraves
   doors/windows L4184
   mouldings/trims L5561
Archive furniture/fittings L843
Armrests L85342
Arris protectors L66383
Arrises L5562
Artificial grass/turf L81312
Artificial ice rinks L81315
Artificial plants L8724
Artificial ski slopes L81314
Artworks L8734
Ash (pulverised fuel) L6222
   sintered L6129
Ashlar stone L3232
Ashtrays L8272
Asphalt L625
   roof L525
Athletics tracks L81313
Atmospheric pressure liquid fuel
   storage tanks L7141
ATMs L85812
Audio communications systems L763
Audio information systems L7611
Audio-visual systems L7613
Auditorium seating L8411
Automated banking
   equipment L85812
Automated guided systems/
   vehicles L775
Automatic document filing/retrieval
   systems L7751
Automatic doors L41109
Avalanche protection products L16
Aviation signals and monitoring
   equipment L2158
Awnings L4212

B

Back boilers L75236
Bains marie L8327
Balcony units L388
Balers L73232
Baling presses L21744
Ball bearing hinges L418304
Ballasts for fluorescent lamps L747364
Balustrades L4421
Bandings L67126
Bank/building society fittings L8581
Banks/dykes L157
Bar reinforcement L3332
Bar sinks L7232
Barbecues L8337
Barbed wire L4431
Barge boards L52941
Barrages L21616
Barrel bolts L418191

Barrel roofs L3822
Barriers L44
   crash L21254
Bars (prestressing) L3342
Bars (reinforcement) L3332
Bars (serving counters) L8341
Barytes L6117
Basins L72104
Bath panels L72102
Bath screens L72109
Bathroom cabinets L8241
Bathroom extract fans L75344
Bathroom furniture/fittings L824
Bathroom suites L721
Baths L72101
Batteries L7411
Beams
   for bridges L21102
   precast concrete L3431
   timber L362
Beanbags L8716
Bearings for bridges L21109
Bedding L8717
Beddings for coverings/
   claddings L553
Bedpan washers L72332
Bedroom furniture L823
Beds L8231
Bedside units L8234
Bellframes L84212
Bells L84212
Belvederes L22109
Benches L8225
Bentonite clay liners L1415
Bibcocks L725113
Bicycle racks L81103
Bidets L72112
Binding agents L62
Bins L8271
Biological attack/damage
   prevention L6818
Biological toilets L721111
Bird baths L81203
Bird boxes L81204
Bird control L6862
Bitumen L625
Blackboards L84541
Blackout blinds L4221
Blade hinges L418308
Blankets
   fireproofing L68112
Blast furnace slag L6111
Blast protection film L41862
Blinds L422
Blockboard L6617
Blocks/blockwork
   for fill L122
   for floors L5332
   for masonry L322
   for strip foundations L313
Boards
   fireproofing L68111
   thermal insulation L68151
   waterproofing L68131
Body care buildings L22107
Body care room units L2223
Boilers L7521
Bollards L81101
Bolt hinges L418305
Bolts
   general purpose L671221
   structural metal L35311
   structural timber L36312
Bolts (sliding)
   for doors L41819
   for windows L41822

M

N

Construction aids

M

Definition Material resources used in production, maintenance and demolition activities, but which are not intended for incorporation into nor for furnishing or equipping construction entities.

Examples Scaffolding, formwork, machines and tools, consumable stores, vehicles, construction products used for temporary works.

Use Classifying trade literature, price lists, hire catalogues, etc. Also organising information about construction aids which may become part of a Health and Safety File.

Concise Table

M1 Pumps for ground water lowering

M11 Mobile pumps
M12 Pumping equipment

M2 Formwork

M21 Wall and floor formwork systems
M22 Form laying equipment, sheets, accessories
M23 Formwork sealing, cleaning products
M24 Formwork scaffolding, supports
M29 Other formwork parts

M3 Scaffolding, shoring, fencing

M31 Complete scaffolding
M32 Scaffolding parts
M33 Shoring, planking and strutting
M34 Temporary fencing structures
M35 Tube straightening equipment
M39 Other scaffolding, shoring, fencing parts

M4 Lifting appliances and conveyors

M41 Cranes
M42 Construction lifts
M43 Winches
M44 Hoists
M45 Conveyors
M46 Lifting trucks
M47 Lifting platforms
M48 Lifting and jacking gear
M49 Other lifting and conveying equipment

M5 Construction vehicles

M51 Complete construction vehicles, general
M52 Excavators, loaders, dredgers
M59 Other construction vehicles

M6 Tunnelling, drilling, compaction

M61 Tunnelling, shafts
M62 Drilling, piling, canal trimming
M63 Compaction equipment
M64 Road, waterway, railway surfacing

M7 Concrete, stone production

M71 Initial production and processing equipment
M72 Further processing and application equipment
M73 Quarrying and tooling equipment
M74 Manufacturing of prefabricated members and blocks

M8 Testing equipment

M81 Concrete testing equipment
M82 Sampling equipment
M83 Weighing machines for construction materials
M84 Weighing machines for vehicles
M85 Pipe testing equipment
M86 Drain testing equipment
M89 Other testing equipment

M9 General equipment

M91 Site accommodation and temporary services
M92 Site equipment
M93 Hand tools
M99 Other general equipment

M1 Pumps for ground water lowering

M2 Formwork

Permanent formwork is at L332.

M23 Formwork sealing, cleaning products

M24 Formwork scaffolding, supports

M241 Telescopic props

M29 Other formwork parts

M11 Mobile pumps

M111 Diaphragm pumps
  1 Single diaphragm pumps
  2 Double diaphragm pumps

M112 Submersible pumps

M113 Induced flow pumps

M114 Centrifugal, self-priming pumps

M115 Semi-rotary pumps

M12 Pumping equipment

M121 Pump hoses
  1 Couplings

M122 Steel pipes
  1 Flanges
  2 Bolts
  3 Joint rings

M123 Bends

M124 Valves

M125 Strainers

M21 Wall and floor formwork systems

M211 Face contact material
  1 Lap plates
  2 Striking pieces
    1 Wrecking strips
  3 Sheeting
    1 Formwork panels
  4 Formwork lining
  5 Draw forms
  6 Beam boxes
  7 Stop end forms

M212 Structural members
  1 Walers
  2 Strongbacks

M213 Box out
  1 Door formers
  2 Window formers
  3 Core forms
  4 Void forms

M22 Form laying equipment, sheets, accessories

M221 Shutters/sheeting

M222 Wedges

M223 Keys

M224 Road forms

M225 Telescopic floor centres

M226 Wrot
  i.e. wrought timber.

M227 Clamps
  1 Column shutter clamps
  2 Beam shutter clamps
  3 Wall shutter clamps
  4 Panel clamps

M228 Formwork ties
  1 Coil ties
  2 Hanger ties
  3 Pigtail ties
  4 Snap ties
  5 Water bar ties
  6 Taper ties
  7 Through ties
  8 Tie sleeves

M229 Access doors and traps

M Construction aids

M3 Scaffolding, shoring, fencing

M31 Complete scaffolding

M311 Prefabricated scaffold
1 Frame scaffold
2 System scaffold

M312 Scaffolding by form
1 Tube and coupler scaffold
2 Timber scaffold
3 Facade scaffold
4 Free standing scaffold
5 Trestle scaffold
6 Suspended scaffold
7 Bracket scaffold
8 Cantilevered scaffold
9 Putlog scaffold

M313 Mobile working towers

M314 Access towers
1 Stair towers
2 Ladder towers

M315 Suspended work platform

M316 Mobile elevating work platform

M32 Scaffolding parts

M321 Frames, framing members
1 Standards
2 Transoms
3 Ledgers
4 Braces
  1 Lateral braces
  2 Longitudinal braces
  3 Plan braces
5 Putlogs
6 Outriggers

M322 Work platforms
1 Adjustable platforms

M323 Cages

M324 Guardrails
1 Handrails
2 Intermediate guardrails
3 Toeboards, guard boards

M325 Access ways
1 Stairways
2 Landings
3 Ladders

M326 Scaffold fittings
1 Couplers
  1 Right angle couplers
  2 Swivel couplers
  3 Parallel couplers
  4 Sleeve couplers
2 Spigots
  1 Loose spigots
  2 Expanding spigots
3 Base plates
4 Scaffold clips
  1 Putlog clips
5 Tie assemblies
  1 Anchorage
  2 Tie members

M327 Stabilisers
1 Ballast

M328 Protection screens
1 Sheeting

M33 Shoring, planking and strutting

M331 Baulk timber

M332 Planking/strutting timber

M333 Adjustable struts

M334 Needles

M335 Dogs

M336 Sole plates

M337 Folding wedges

M34 Temporary fencing structures

Permanent fencing is at L4411.

M341 Fencing supports

M342 Fencing panels, boarding, fencing chestnut

M343 Temporary hoardings

M35 Tube straightening equipment

M39 Other scaffolding, shoring, fencing parts

M4 Lifting appliances and conveyors

M41 Cranes

M411 Cranes by type
Tower cranes are at M412.
1 Turret cranes
2 Truck-mounted cranes
3 Rough-terrain (RT) and all-terrain (AT) cranes
4 Mobile cranes
5 Track-laying cranes
6 Cranes for mounting on vehicle chassis
7 Frame cranes
8 Portal cranes
9 Cranes with telescopic jib

M412 Tower cranes
1 Mobile tower cranes
2 Static tower cranes
3 Rail mounted tower cranes
4 Climbing tower cranes
5 Trolley jib tower cranes
6 Luffing jib tower cranes

M413 Other cranes

M414 Crane equipment
1 Tipping buckets
2 Rubbish buckets
3 Concrete skips
4 Tower crane track etc.
5 Crane grabs
  1 Crane grabs, excavating
  2 Crane grabs, rehandling
6 Demolition balls
7 Other crane equipment

M42 Construction lifts

M421 Lift platforms

M422 Lift cages

M423 Lifting mechanisms

M424 Safety limiters

M425 Bottom/landing gates

M426 Other lift equipment

M43 Winches

Includes hoist winches, draw winches, other construction winches.

M431 Double drum friction winches

M432 Single drum winches

M433 Other winch equipment

M44 Hoists

M441 Scaffold hoists

M442 Mobile hoists
For use with goods only.

M443 Rack and pinion hoists, single use
For use with goods only.

M444 Rack and pinion hoists, dual use
For use with goods and passengers.

M445 Lorry loaders

M446 Other hoist equipment

M45 Conveyors

M451 Belt conveyors, belt weighers
1 Conveyor belts
2 Steep-incline conveyors
3 Apron conveyors
4 Link conveyors
5 Weighing conveyors
6 Screw conveyors
7 Bucket conveyors
8 Factory conveyors
9 Vibrators for material conveying and pneumatic conveyor lines

M452 Bucket railways

M453 Other conveying equipment

M46 Lifting trucks

Lifting trucks, including fork-lift trucks, may have 2 or 4 wheel drive, and may be suitable for rough terrain.

M461 Lift trucks

M462 Manual lift trucks

M463 Portal lift trucks

M47 Lifting platforms

M471 Self-propelled platforms

M472 Trailer mounted/portable platforms

M473 Scissor lifts

M474 Telescopic platforms

M475 Vehicle-mounted platforms

M48 Lifting and jacking gear

M481 Pipe winches
1 Pipe winch with shear legs
2 Pipe winch with gantry

M482 Chain blocks

M483 Pull lift

M484 Chains

M485 Slings/brothers

M486 Ropes

M487 Wires

M488 Jacks
1 Hydraulic jack
2 Ratchet jack

M49 Other lifting and conveying equipment

M5 Construction vehicles

M51 Complete construction vehicles, general

M511 Lorries
1 Fixed body lorries
2 Haulers
3 Articulated lorries

M512 Dumper trucks, tipper lorries and equipment
1 Tipper lorries
  1 Side tippers
  2 Front tippers
  3 Multi-bucket tippers
  4 Three-way tippers
  5 Rolling tippers
  6 Rear tippers
  7 Gravity tippers
  8 Hydraulic tippers
2 Dumper trucks
  1 Rigid dumpers
  2 Articulated dumpers
3 Tipper chassis
4 Shuttle train
5 Turntable skip

M513 Tractors
1 Agricultural-type tractor
2 Tractor with dozer
3 Tractor with bull/angle dozer
4 Tractor with dozer and ripper attachment
5 Tractor loading shovel
  1 Tractor loading shovel with back hoe equipment
  2 Tractor loading shovel with four in one attachment
  3 Tractor-mounted loading shovel with ripper attachment
6 Motor grader
7 Motorised scraper
  1 Motorised elevating scraper
8 Tractor shovel

M514 Semi-trailer type tractor trucks

M515 Truck chassis for special superstructures

M516 Vehicle superstructures and trailers
1 Tanker vehicles
2 Silo vehicles
3 Low-loaders
4 Semi-trailers
5 Trailers
  1 Tipping trailers
6 Heavy-duty trailers
7 Special vehicles
  1 Vans
  2 Pick-up trucks
  3 Passenger/goods cross-country vehicles
  4 Self-propelled road sweepers/cleaners
  5 Road sweepers with gully emptiers
8 Communal vehicles
  1 Station wagons
  2 Coaches/buses

M517 Water supply vehicles and equipment
1 Water storage tank trailer
2 Self-propelled water tanker

M518 Fuel supply vehicles and equipment
1 Fuel storage tank
2 Fuel storage tank trailer
3 Self-propelled fuel tanker
4 LPG cylinders

M52 Excavators, loaders, dredgers

M521 Excavators
1 Tracked excavators
  1 Hydraulic track-laying excavators
  2 Cable track excavators
2 Mobile excavators
  1 Hydraulic mobile excavators
  2 Cable mobile excavators
3 Telescopic excavators
4 Trenchers
  1 Bucket trenchers
  2 Pipelayers
  3 Boom-type trenching machines
  4 Highway trenchers
5 Bucket wheel excavators
6 Full circle slew excavators
7 Mini excavators
8 Rope-operated excavators

M522 Combined excavator loaders

M523 Dredging boats and equipment
1 Suction dredgers, cutter dredgers
2 Grab-type dredgers
3 Bucket-chain dredgers
4 Armoured pumps
5 Buckhow diggers and scrapers

M524 Loaders
1 Track-laying loaders
2 Wheel-loaders
3 Skid steer loaders
4 Crawler loaders
5 Digging arm loaders

M525 Scrapers
See also M5235 Buckhow diggers and scrapers.
1 Elevating scrapers
2 Track-laying scrapers
3 Four-wheeled scrapers
4 Scraper systems, gravel extraction

M526 Dozers and graders
1 Dozers
  1 Wheeled dozers
  2 Crawler dozers
  3 Tracked dozers
  4 Angling dozers
  5 Straight dozers
2 Road graders

M527 Attachments for excavators, scrapers, dozers, etc.
1 Draglines
2 Backacters
3 Percussion breakers
4 Backhoe loaders
5 Rippers
  1 Hinge type rippers
  2 Parallelogram type rippers
  3 Variable geometry rippers
6 Shovels
  1 Face shovels
7 Graders
8 Trenchers

M528 Excavator mats

M59 Other construction vehicles

M6 Tunnelling, drilling, compaction

M61 Tunnelling, shafts

M611 Cutting machines
1 Partial cutting machines
2 Full cutting machines
  1 Thrustboring equipment

M612 Shields
1 Tunnel shields
2 Cutter shields

M613 Rough press equipment

M614 Drilling vehicles and explosives vehicles

M615 Transport and conveyor systems

M616 Ventilation and dust extraction

M617 Lining systems for tunnels

M618 Blasting equipment
1 Explosives
2 Detonators

M619 Other tunnelling equipment

M62 Drilling, piling, canal trimming

M621 Drilling machines and plant
1 Drilling machines for soil exploration
2 Core cutting machines
3 Drilling machines for foundations piles
4 Drilling machines for post and mast holes
5 Well drilling systems
6 Suction drilling systems
7 Drilling vehicles
8 Pressure drilling machines
9 Hammer-action drills

M622 Pile drivers (rammers) and pulling tools
1 Double-acting piling hammers
2 Drop hammers
3 Impulse hammers
4 Internal drop hammers for use with cased piles
5 Extractors
6 Diesel hammer
7 Vibrating hammer/extractor
8 Piling accessories
  1 Pile helmets
  2 Dollies
  3 Hanging leaders

M623 Canal sheeting equipment
1 Trench sheeting equipment
  1 Trench struts and sheets
  2 Adjustable steel trench struts
  3 Steel trench sheets
2 Canal sheeting
3 Canal shoring
4 Trench ring lifters
5 Sliding-blade sheeting

M624 Hydraulic pipe pushers

M625 Specialist piling/drilling plant
1 Auger piling plant
2 Diaphragm walling plant

M63 Compaction equipment

M631 Rollers
1 Vibrating rollers
  1 Double vibrating rollers
  2 Tandem vibrating rollers
  3 Trailer vibration rollers
  4 Combination vibration rollers
2 Roller trains
3 Pneumatic tyre rollers
4 Static three-wheeled and tandem rollers
5 Sheepsfoot rollers
6 Single rollers
7 Twin rollers
  1 Twin rollers with seat and steering wheel
8 Deadweight rollers
  1 Pavement rollers

M632 Rammers
1 Vibration rammers
2 Jumping rammers

M633 Soil compactors
1 Sheepsfoot compactors

M64 Road, waterway, railway surfacing

M641 Road construction equipment
1 Soil stabilisation machines
2 Concrete road finishers and spreaders
3 Asphalt, mastic and tar preparation equipment
  1 Processing, drying and mixing installations for asphalt road construction
    Includes mobile, transportable and stationary installations.
  2 Asphalt road finishers
  3 Mastic finishers
  4 Tar and mastic heaters
    Includes asphalt burners.
  5 Tar sprayers
  6 Heatable bitumen storage tanks
4 Spreaders
  1 Stone spreaders
    Includes chipping applicators, gritters.
  2 Asphalt spreaders
  3 Coated macadam spreaders
  4 Spreaders for soil stabilisation
5 Joint cutters
  1 Joint matchers
  2 Joint formers
6 Road milling cutters
7 Gas infra-red units, road drying equipment
8 Paving stone laying machines

M642 Canal bank grading, compacting, concreting and asphalting machinery, canal bed cleaning machines

M643 Track-laying machines

M644 Machines for road repair and maintenance
1 Asphalt pavement equipment
  1 Road surface rippers
    Includes asphalt road burners.
  2 Asphalt pavement reshapers
  3 Asphalt pavement recycling machines
2 Joint cleaning and filling machines
3 Repair kits
4 Stone and sand spreaders
5 Road marking machines
6 Sweeping machines
7 Slope mowing machines
8 Scarifiers

M645 Planers
1 Heater planers
2 Cold planers

M7 Concrete, stone production

M71 Initial production and processing equipment

M711 Complete plant
1 Complete plant for the cement, lime, gypsum, trass and chalk industry
2 Complete plant for the sand, clay, gravel and broken stone industry

M712 Breakers, crushers, mills
1 Stone breakers
2 Brick crushers
3 Gyratory crushers
4 Impact-type crushers
5 Hammer crushers
6 Roller crushers
7 Mills
  1 Impact mills
  2 Hammer mills
  3 Roller mills
  4 Tube mills
  5 Vibrating grinding mills

M713 Screening and sorting plant
1 Vibrating screens
2 Circular vibratory screens
3 Eccentric vibratory screens
4 Linear vibratory screens
5 Screens with electromagnetic drive

M714 Washing machines, scoops for sand, gravel, etc.

M715 Silos for gravel and broken stone

M716 Drying installations for the stone and aggregate industry

M717 Dust extraction plant

M718 Stackers and reclaimers

M719 Recycling plant for construction debris

M72 Further processing and application equipment

M721 Concrete and mortar mixers
1 Rotary mixers
2 Concrete processing systems
  1 Concrete processing systems with horizontal aggregate feed
  2 Concrete processing systems with vertical aggregate feed
3 Metering and weighing equipment
4 Hand scrapers, scraper installations
5 Silos for cement and aggregates
6 Mixers by type of drum
  1 Open drum mixers with hopper
  2 Open drum mixers without hopper
  3 Closed drum mixers
  4 Reversing drum mixers with hopper, weigher and feed shovel
  5 Tilting drum mixers

M722 Concrete transport, concrete and mortar conveying
1 Mobile mixers
2 Equipment for washing out concrete residues
3 Concrete agitators
4 Concrete and mortar buckets
5 Concrete pumps and equipment
  1 Lorry mounted concrete pumps with boom
  2 Piping
  3 Flexible distributor hose
  4 Shut off pipe sections
  5 Pipe cleaning equipment
6 Concrete truck mixer/agitators with separate engine with mechanical/hydraulic drive to drum
7 Mortar/screed pumps
  1 Mortar/screed pump hoses

M723 Concrete compaction and finishing equipment
1 Concrete vibrators
  1 External vibrators
    Includes vibrators applied or fixed to formwork.
  2 Immersion vibrators
    Includes poker vibrators.
  3 Surface vibrators
  4 Tamper vibrators
2 Concrete finishing equipment
  1 Power floats
  2 Power trowels
  3 Screed boards

M724 Attachments for concrete and mortar plant
1 Power driven loading shovels
2 Aggregate feed aprons

M725 Batching plant
1 Silos
  1 Aerated silos
2 Autofeed equipment
3 Weighgear
  1 Hydraulic cement weighgear
  2 Electronic weighgear
4 Screw discharge gear
5 Batch loaders

M726 Grouting equipment
1 Grout mixers
2 Roller type grout mixers
3 Loading hoppers with weighgear and loading shovel
4 Grout mixers/pumps
5 Grouting machines with pump and hopper
6 Grout pumps
7 Agitating tanks for use with grout pumps

M727 Concrete and mortar application
1 Spreaders
2 Concrete guns, concrete injectors
3 Gunite equipment
4 Rendering machines

M728 Measuring equipment for concrete manufacture

M73 Quarrying and tooling equipment

M731 Stone drilling machines

M732 Stone cleaving machines and equipment

M733 Stone sawing equipment
1 Reciprocating sawing machines
2 Cutting-out saws

M734 Abrasive cutting off machines

M735 Slab cutting machines and equipment

M736 Milling machines

M737 Sanding and polishing machines and lines

M738 Grouting machines for cast stone slabs

M739 Diamond tools

M74 Manufacturing of prefabricated members and blocks

M741 Concrete block, pipe, kerb and tile machines and plant
01 Concrete block machines with support boards
02 Concrete block machines without support boards
03 Moulds for the concrete block industry
04 Presses
  1 Concrete slab presses
  2 Revolving presses
05 Vibrating tables
06 Machines for washing concrete to expose the aggregate, paper lining machines and accessories
07 Concrete pipe machines
08 Centrifugal casting machines
09 Kerb stone machines
10 Step machines
11 Roof tile machines
12 Synthetic resin concrete casting machines
13 Hardening plant

M742 Plant for the manufacture of large-format precast concrete elements
1 Battery formwork
  Other formwork is at M21.
2 Tilting tables for precast concrete elements
3 Prestressed concrete systems
4 Slip finishers for prestressed concrete beams and slabs
5 Finishers for walls and ceilings

M743 Transport equipment for the concrete block industry
1 Automatic transfer systems
2 Grabs and loading devices for concrete blocks
3 Vehicles for feeding concrete block machines
4 Slab stacking devices
5 Block packaging, binding and shrink foil plant
6 Pallets

M744 Plant for the manufacture of sand-lime bricks

M745 Machines and plant for the manufacture of lightweight concrete blocks and elements

M746 Machines and plant for the manufacture of lightweight building boards and pipes

M8 Testing equipment

M81 Concrete testing equipment

M82 Sampling equipment

M83 Weighing machines for construction materials

M84 Weighing machines for vehicles

M85 Pipe testing equipment

M86 Drain testing equipment

M861 Sewer test and inspection equipment

M89 Other testing equipment

Construction aids

M9 General equipment

M91 Site accomodation and temporary services

M911 Site accommodation
1 Site huts, containers and static caravans
  1 Office fittings
  2 Mess room fittings
  3 Store fittings
2 Motor caravans
3 Toilet vehicles and cabins
  1 Toilet units

M912 Installations and equipment for winter construction
1 Construction drying equipment
2 Steam generators, water heaters
3 Space heaters
4 Watchman's heaters

M913 Site lighting equipment
1 Warning lamps
2 Portable floodlights
3 Tilley lamps
4 Watchman's lamps

M914 Site electrical equipment
1 Site electrical distributors
2 Cable laying machines and equipment
3 Cable and pipeline detectors

M915 Power generating units
1 Power generating units, stationery
2 Power generating units, mobile

M916 Frequency and voltage transformers

M917 Drainage equipment
1 Drainage rods
2 Expanding drain stoppers

M918 Rubbish collection and disposal equipment
1 Rubbish chutes
2 Skips

M92 Site equipment

M921 Surveying and measuring equipment
1 Levels
  1 Dumpy levels
  2 Auto levels
  3 Engineers' precise auto levels
  4 Tilting levels
  5 Theodolites
  6 Water levels
  7 Levelling staffs
  8 Spirit levels
2 Other surveying equipment
  1 Ranging rods, poles
  2 Tripods
  3 Staffs
  4 Optical plummets
  5 Centring rods
  6 Measuring telescopes
  7 Electro-magnetic distance measuring instruments (EDM instruments)
  8 Direction indicating devices
  9 Surface indicating devices
3 Measuring equipment
  1 Measuring tape
  Includes tape tensioners.
  2 Folding rules
  3 Measuring rod
  4 Plumb line
  5 Clinometer
  6 Profile boards
  7 Sight rails
  8 Boning rods
  9 Tachometer

M922 Welding equipment
1 Underwater welding equipment
2 Thermic boring equipment
3 Welding electrodes
4 Oxy-acetylene cutting and welding sets
5 Diesel welding sets
6 Welding accessories
  1 Head screens
  2 Helmets

M923 Protective equipment
1 Signals for construction sites
  1 Warning signs
2 Personal safety equipment
  Welding safety equipment is at M9226.
  1 Protective nets
  2 Safety harnesses
  3 Goggles
3 Road works equipment
  1 Traffic control lamps
    1 Traffic lights
    2 Danger lamps
    3 Flashing traffic warning lamps
  2 Barrier trestles
  3 Crossing plates
  4 Road cones
  5 Flashing bollards
  6 Speed deterrents

M923 3 *continued*
  7 Traffic information signs
  Permanent road signs are at L2152.
    1 Traffic control signs
    2 Traffic warning signs
    3 Illuminated traffic information signs
    Includes electronic traffic information signs.

M924 DPC equipment
1 Caulking gun
2 High pressure injection equipment
3 Low pressure injection equipment
4 Gravity feed equipment
5 Electro-osmosis equipment

M925 Cleaning and surface preparation equipment
1 High pressure and steam jet cleaners
2 Low pressure cleaning machines
3 Underwater cleaning equipment
4 Blasting machines and equipment

M926 Compressors, compressed-air machines and equipment
1 Compressors
  1 Lorry-mounted compressors
  2 Tractor-mounted compressors
2 Compressed-air machines and equipment
  1 Air hoses
  2 Mufflers
  3 Tool silencers
  4 Air receivers

M927 Steel reinforcement cutting and bending plant and equipment
1 Bar bending machines
2 Bar shearing machines
3 Bar cropper machines

M928 Dehumidifiers

M929 Other site equipment
1 Tarpaulins
2 Ladders, general
3 Loading rails
4 Buckets

M93 Hand tools

M931 Saws
1 Hand saws
  1 Coping saws
  2 Fretsaws
  3 Compass saws
  4 Drywall saws
  5 Panel saws
  6 Hacksaws
  7 Back saws
  8 Flooring saws
  9 Bow saws
2 Power saws
  1 Circular saws
  2 Brick saws
  3 Chain saws
  4 Band saws
  5 Mitre saws
  6 Jig saws

M932 Pipe work equipment
1 Pipe cutters
2 Pipe benders
3 Pipe defrosting equipment
4 Pipe threading equipment
5 Flaring tools
6 Pairs of footprints
7 Pipe wrenches
  Also known as stillson wrenches.
8 Plumber's furnace

M933 Hammers
1 Bricklayer's hammers
2 Carpenter's hammers
3 Bush hammers
4 Club hammers
5 Sledge hammers
6 Chipping hammers
7 Rotary hammers
8 Riveting hammers
9 Demolition hammers

M934 Hand-held drills and equipment
1 Rotary drills
2 Rock drills
3 Reversible drills
4 Wheelbraces
5 Drill bits
6 Drill rods
7 Pipe drilling tackle
8 Diamond drilling and chasing equipment
9 Drill stands

M935 Painting, insulation application equipment
1 Paint brushes
2 Paint rollers
3 Paint kettles
4 Spraying equipment for paints and insulation
5 Insulation injection equipment
6 Paint metering systems

M936 Barrows
1 Hand barrows
2 Powered barrows

M937 Digging tools
1 Spades
2 Clay spits
3 Picks

M938 Other hand tools
1 Screwdrivers
  1 Ratchet screwdrivers
2 Trowels
  1 Angle trowels
  2 Gauging trowels
  3 Laying-on trowels
3 Floats
  1 Devil floats
  2 Cross-grained floats
4 Bolt cutters
5 Spanners
  Includes wrenches.
6 Allen keys
7 Levering bars
  1 Crowbars
  2 Pinch bars
    Includes case openers, claw bars, jemmies, wrecking bars.

M939 Other electrical tools
1 Sanders
  1 Orbital sanders
  2 Belt sanders
2 Grinders
  1 Angle grinders
  2 Bench grinders
  3 Straight grinders
3 Polishers
4 Planers
5 Routers
6 Scabblers
7 Breakers
8 Strimmers

M99 Other general equipment

Properties and characteristics

N

Definition	Properties, characteristics and other factors concerning physical objects of all kinds, including construction products, work sections, elements, whole buildings and other constructions.
Examples	Tolerances, size, shape, fire, explosion, change in use, user groups, ergonomics, change.
Use	The classification of subjects relating to properties and characteristics. The arrangement of information about construction products in technical documents.

Concise Table

N1 Descriptive

N11 Composition
N12 Production
N13 Assembly, connecting and fixing
N14 Accessories
N15 Shape, size, tolerance
N16 Mass, density
N17 Appearance etc.
N19 Other descriptive properties and characteristics

N2 Context, environment

N21 Regional
N22 Meteorological
N23 Topographical
N24 Physiographic, geological
N25 Relating to modified environments

N3 Performance

N31 Structural, mechanical
N32 Fire, explosion
N33 Interactions of matter
N34 Biological
N35 Thermal
N36 Optical
N37 Acoustic
N38 Electric, magnetic, electromagnetic radiation
N39 Energy, other performance

N4 Applications, activities

N41 User activities
Use this section for user activities by combining this class number with those from the Facilities table, e.g. N41:D32 Office work
N42 Proper use, limitations on use
N43 Suitability, efficiency, effectiveness
N44 Usefulness, obsolescence, degree of utilisation
N45 Re-use, change in use, adaptability, flexibility
N46 Consumption, waste, conservation
N47 Mis-use, wrong use, mistakes in use
N48 Failure, deficiency in use, defects
N49 Other aspects

N5 Users, resources

N51 User groups, communities
N52 Society, sociological characteristics
N53 People, users
N54 Physical and mental properties and characteristics
N55 Non-human 'users'
N56 Resources
N59 Other

N6 Ease of use, workability

N61 Ease of storing
N62 Ease of dismantling
N63 Ease of moving
N64 Ease of cutting
N65 Ease of drilling
N66 Ease of placing, connecting
N67 Ease of altering
N68 Ease of cleaning
N69 Other

N7 Operation and maintenance

N71 Method of operation
N72 Maintenance
N73 Overhaul and repair
N74 Modification etc.
N75 Restoration, replacement, etc.
N79 Other

N8 Change, movement, stability

N81 Associative change
N82 Dissociative change
N83 Transfer
N84 Extensive change
N85 Limited change, stability
N86 Gradual change
N87 Quality change
N88 Causes, effects of change

N9 Other properties and characteristics

N1 Descriptive

N11 Composition

N111 Constituent materials

N112 Parts, components

N12 Production

N121 Method of manufacture

N122 Productivity

N123 Automation

N13 Assembly, connecting and fixing

N131 On-site

N132 Off-site

N133 Loose fit

N134 Close fit

N135 Adhesion

N136 Connection

N137 Fastening

N138 Locking

N14 Accessories

N15 Shape, size, tolerance

N151 Shape, geometry, layout

N152 Size
1 Dimensional coordination, modular coordination
2 Volume, capacity
3 Area
4 Vertical dimensions
  1 Height
  2 Altitude
  3 Elevation
  4 Depth
  5 Cover
  6 Gradient, slope, fall
5 Longitudinal dimensions, length
  1 Length
  2 Span
  3 Distance
  4 Length of perimeter
6 Latitudinal dimensions, thickness
  1 Thickness
  2 Diameter, radius, bore
  3 Gauge
7 Scale, relative dimension
8 Change in shape, size
  1 Expansion
  2 Shrinkage
  3 Movement
9 Tolerance, fit, accuracy

N153 Units of measurement/ dimensional systems
Includes metric system, metrication.

N16 Mass, density

N161 Mass (weight)

N162 Density

N17 Appearance etc.

N171 Style, form, aesthetic quality

N172 Texture, feel
1 Roughness
2 Smoothness
3 Flatness, evenness
4 Pattern

N173 Colour, visibility

N174 Opacity

N175 Smell, odour

N176 Taste

N177 Aural qualities

N19 Other

N2 Context, environment

N21 Regional

N211 Polar

N212 Temperate

N213 Sub-tropical

N214 Tropical

N22 Meteorological

N221 Climate

N222 Sunshine

N223 Wind

N224 Storms, lightning

N225 Precipitation
1 Rain
2 Hail
3 Snow

N226 Weather tightness, proofing

N227 Weathering

N229 Others

N23 Topographical

N24 Physiographic, geological

N241 Avalanches

N242 Tides

N243 Droughts

N244 Floods

N245 Volcanic eruptions

N246 Earthquakes

N247 Subsidence

N25 Relating to modified environments

N251 Overshadowing

N252 Wind effects
e.g. around tall buildings.

N253 Traffic

N254 Air pollution

N3 Performance

N31 Structural, mechanical

N311 Overall strength/stability of structures; effects of/resistance to various types of loading
1 Static loading, deformation
2 Live loading
3 Horizontal loading, wind loading
4 Thermal loading
5 Seismic loading
6 Impact loading
7 Penetration
8 Subsidence, settlement
9 Other

N312 Strength of materials, components of structures
1 Tensile strength
2 Compressive strength
3 Shear strength
4 Bending strength

N313 Toughness, resistance to cracking

N314 Hardness, resistance to surface indentation/scratching

N315 Fatigue resistance

N316 Creep resistance

N317 Elasticity

N318 Friction, adhesion

N319 Other structural, mechanical properties and characteristics
1 Vibration properties and characteristics

N32 Fire, explosion

N321 Fire types, sources, severity

N322 Reaction of materials to fire
1 Combustibility
2 Total heat emitted, calorific value
3 Rate of heat release, fire load
4 Ignitability
  1 Flame impingement
  2 Thermal irradiance
  3 Flash point of liquids
5 Surface spread of flame
6 Flame propagation
7 Smoke/gas release
8 Smoke/gas propagation

N323 Fire resistance (structures)
1 Maintenance of loadbearing capacity
2 Maintenance of integrity
3 Maintenance of insulation
4 Increasing fire resistance by means of a surface coating, encasement
5 Increasing fire resistance by changing choice of material
6 Increasing fire resistance by increasing thickness of elements

N324 Fire safety, protection properties and characteristics (basic)
Excludes fire resistance (see N323).
1 Means of escape
2 Internal fire spread (linings)
3 Internal fire spread (structure), fire compartmentation, fire barriers
4 External fire spread
5 Access and facilities for the fire service
6 Fire endurance

N325 Fire engineering, further fire safety properties and characteristics
1 Fire prevention
2 Fire detection, warning
3 Venting/control of smoke and fumes
4 Control of rate of growth of fire
5 Extinguishing fire with sprinkler systems, fire extinguishers
6 Training in fire safety
7 Maintaining fire safety systems

N326 Explosions

N327 Fire and explosion damage, salvage

N329 Other fire, explosion properties and characteristics

N33 Interactions of matter

Properties and characteristics relating to interactions of matter.

N331 Properties and characteristics of air, gases
1 Air quality, cleanliness of air
2 Humidity
3 Velocity of air
4 Air pressure, pressurisation
5 Draughts

N332 Interactions between air/gas and solids
Excludes water vapour.
1 Air tightness
2 Air leakage
3 Permeability to gas, permeability to pollutants
4 Air infiltration

N333 Interactions between water vapour and solids
1 Water vapour penetration
2 Water vapour permeability
3 Condensation, surface
4 Condensation, interstitial
5 Hygroscopy, moisture absorption
6 Hygrometric expansion
7 Moisture resistance

N334 Interactions between liquid water and solids
1 Liquid water absorption
2 Imperviousness to water
3 Permeability to water
4 Resistance to corrosion
5 Water leakage

N335 Interactions between the weather/ground conditions and solids
1 Frost resistance
2 Resistance to penetration of driving rain and snow
3 Resistance to rising damp

N336 Wastes, pollution, harmful effects of matter
1 Solid waste
2 Liquid waste
3 Effectiveness in disposal of liquid waste
4 Gaseous waste
5 Non-release of foul air
6 Particulate discharge
7 Release of volatile organic compounds
8 Odour
9 Toxicity, chemical safety

N339 Other interactions of matter

N34 Biological

Susceptibility to/precautions against the following:

N341 Human accidental damage, vandalism, theft

N342 Animals, birds, insects

N343 Harmful bacteria, viruses, etc.
1 Legionnaires' disease

N344 Growth of fungi, plants

N35 Thermal

N351 Heat types, sources

N352 Thermal insulation

N353 Thermal transfer
1 Thermal transmittance (U value), thermal transmissivity
2 Surface coefficient
3 Thermal conductance (C value), thermal conductivity (k value)
4 Thermal resistance (R value), thermal resistivity (r value)
5 Convection
6 Radiation
7 Thermal emission, absorption

N354 Heat capacity, specific heat

N355 Heat loss, gain
1 Solar heat gain
2 Heat loss characteristics

N356 Temperature
1 Room temperature
2 Temperature of outside air
3 Melting point, freezing point
4 Boiling point

N357 Thermal expansion

N359 Other thermal properties and characteristics

N36 Optical

N361 Light types, sources
1 Natural light
2 Artificial light
  1 Wide spectrum artificial light
3 Combined natural and
  artificial light

N362 Light insulation
1 Light protection, proofing
2 Light tightness

N363 Light transmission, absorption, emission
1 Light transmission
  1 Spectral transmission
    characteristics
2 Light absorption
3 Light emission

N364 Light reflection, polarisation, refraction
1 Reflection factor, reflectance,
  reflectivity
2 Fully reflecting, mirrored
3 Non reflecting, matt
4 Degree, type of polarisation
5 Refractive index

N365 Brightness, luminous intensity
1 Luminance

N366 Glare
1 Glare index

N367 Transparency

N368 Visibility

N369 Other optical properties and characteristics

N37 Acoustic

N371 Noise types, sources

N372 Acoustic insulation, protection
1 Protection against airborne
  noise from outside
2 Protection against noise from
  another internal space
3 Protection against
  structure-borne and impact
  noise
4 Protection against equipment
  noise
5 Protection against reverberant
  noise

N373 Sound transmission, resistance, absorption
1 Noise absorption coefficient
2 Noise transmission factor

N374 Sound reflection

N375 Noise levels
1 Noise level in decibels
2 Loud (high noise level)
3 Quiet (low noise level)
4 Speech intelligibility rating

N376 Noise frequency

N379 Other acoustic properties and characteristics

N38 Electric, magnetic, electromagnetic radiation

N381 Electricity types, sources
1 Alternating currents (AC)
2 Direct currents (DC)
3 Static electricity

N382 Electrical insulation, protection, safety
1 Electrical insulation
2 Electrical protection
3 Electrical safety, avoidance of
  shocks

N383 Electrical conduction, resistance
1 Conductivity
2 Conductance
3 Resistivity
4 Resistance
5 Admittance

N384 Electrical ionisation

N385 Other electrical measures
1 Voltage (volts)
2 Current (amps)
3 Power (watts)
4 Capacitance
5 Dielectric constant
6 Electric field strength

N386 Magnetic properties and characteristics

N387 Electromagnetic radiation, radioactivity properties and characteristics
Excludes visible electromagnetic radiation.
1 Infrared radiation
2 Ultraviolet radiation
3 Radioactivity

N389 Other electric, magnetic, electromagnetic properties and characteristics

N39 Energy, other performance

N391 Energy types, measures
1 Kinetic energy
2 Potential energy
3 Calories
4 Joules

N392 Energy output

N393 Energy demand, input

N394 Energy efficiency

N395 Other energy properties and characteristics

N396/9
*Other performance properties
and characteristics*

N396 Compatibility

N397 Durability

N398 Side-effects

N399 Other

N4 Applications, activities

N41 User activities

Use this section for user activities by combining this class number with those from Table D Facilities. The main classes which will result from this process are listed below, but it is possible to create more classes by using the fine detail of the Facilities table.

N41:D1 Travel, transport, etc. activities
1 Rail travel
2 Road travel
3 Water travel
4 Air travel
5 Communication
6 Power supply, mineral supply
  1/4 Power generation and supply
  5/8 Mineral extraction and supply
7 Water supply; disposal
  1 Water supply
  2 Wet waste, sewage treatment
  3 Refuse disposal
  4 Mineral waste disposal

N41:D2 Industrial activities
6 Agriculture
7 Manufacturing, production

N41:D3 Administration, commerce, protection
1 Official administration
2 Office work
3 Commerce
4 Trading
7 Protection
  1 Rescue/aid
  4 Law enforcement
  5 Military
  6 Detention

N41:D4 Medical care, health care, welfare
1 Medical care
2 Primary health care
4 Welfare
6 Animal welfare

N41:D5 Recreation
1 Refreshment
2 Entertainment
3 Social recreation
4 Swimming
6 Sport
8 Amusement, play, tourism
  1 Gambling
  3 Amusement
  4 Tourism
  5 Play
  7 Using parks, gardens

N41:D6 Worship, religion

N41:D7 Education, science, information access and study
1 Education
2 Further education
3 Science, computing
  1 Computing
4 Assembly
5 Exhibition, display
6 Information access, study

N41:D8 Living, rest, sleeping
2 Living, rest
3 Sleeping

N41:D9 Other
1 Circulation
2 Reception, waiting
4 Sanitary, cleaning, changing
6 Storage
7 Control, servicing

N42 Proper use, limitations on use

N43 Suitability, efficiency, effectiveness

N44 Usefulness, obsolescence, degree of utilisation

N45 Re-use, change in use, adaptability, flexibility

N46 Consumption, waste, conservation

N461 Consumption

N462 Waste

N463 Conservation

N47 Mis-use, wrong use, mistakes in use

N48 Failure, deficiency in use, defects

N49 Other aspects

N5 Users, resources

N51 User groups, communities

N511 Hereditary groups
1 Families
2 Tribes
4 Races

N512 Organised groups
1 Households
2 Societies
3 Associations
4 Nations

N513 Unorganised groups
1 Crowds
2 Masses
3 Herds

N52 Society, sociological characteristics

N521 Demography

N522 Customs

N523 Morals, ethics

N524 Social economics

N525 Social psychology

N53 People, users

N531 Children
1 Babies, infants
2 Adolescents, teenagers

N532 Adults
1 Parents
2 Old people

N533 Females/males
1 Females, women
2 Males, men

N534 People according to marital status
1 Single, unmarried
2 Married
3 Divorced

N535 People with special needs
1 Sick people
2 Physically handicapped people
3 Mentally handicapped people
4 Addicts

N536 People according to economic status, other status
1 Rich, high income
2 Poor, low income
3 Landlords
4 Tenants, occupiers
5 Homeless
6 Employers
7 Employees

N537 People according to function, work
1 Manual workers
2 Administrative workers
3 Professionals
4 Passengers
5 Visitors

N539 Other people, users

N54 Physical and mental

N541 Body properties and characteristics
1 Anatomical properties and characteristics, posture
2 Ergonomics
3 Physiological properties and characteristics
4 Anthropometrics

N542 Comfort, convenience

N543 Health, hygiene properties and characteristics
1 Illness, disease
3 Nutrition
4 Cleanliness
5 Sanitation
7 Stress

N544 Safety and security properties and characteristics

N549 Other physical and mental properties and characteristics

N55 Non-human 'users'

N551 Animals

N552 Plants

N553 Machines

N56 Resources

N561 Natural resources

N562 Man-made resources

N59 Other

N6 Ease of use, workability

N61 Ease of storing

N62 Ease of dismantling

Includes demountability and detachability.

N63 Ease of moving

N64 Ease of cutting

N65 Ease of drilling

N66 Ease of placing, connecting

N661 Ease of coating
1 Consistency
2 Spreadability
3 Hiding power
4 Drying

N662 Ease of joining, fixing
1 Adhesiveness
2 Cohesiveness
3 Weldability
4 Nailability

N67 Ease of altering

Includes adaptability, adjustability, interchangeability.

N68 Ease of cleaning

N69 Other

N7 Operation and maintenance

N71 Method of operation

N72 Maintenance

N721 Routine servicing

N722 Cleaning

N73 Overhaul and repair

N74 Modification etc.

N741 Alteration

N742 Adaptation

N743 Modification

N744 Conversion

N75 Restoration, replacement, etc.

N751 Restoration

N752 Reconstruction

N753 Renovation

N754 Renewal

N755 Replacement

N79   Other

N84   Extensive change

N841   Disturbance

N842   Transformation

N843   Renewal

N844   Substitution

N845   Revolution

N81   Associative change

N811   Integration

N812   Acquisition

N813   Concentration

N814   Addition

N815   Absorption

N85   Limited change, stability

N851   Stability

N82   Dissociative change

N821   Disintegration

N822   Separation

N823   Differentiation

N824   Subtraction, removal, extraction

N825   Leakage

N826   Emission

N827   Distribution

N86   Gradual change

N861   Evolution, development, growth

N862   Devolution, decline, ageing

N863   Maturing

N864   Curing

N83   Transfer

N831   Movement

N832   Rhythm

N87   Quality change

N871   Improvement
   1 Modernisation
   2 Reinforcement
   3 Toughening
   4 Stiffening
   5 Purification

N872   Deterioration
   1 Dilapidation
   2 Dereliction
   3 Decay
   4 Wear
   5 Damage
   6 Breakage
   7 Weakening

Materials

P

Definition	Substances and materials from which construction products, elements or entities may be made.
Examples	Timber, cement, plastics, stone.
Use	Classifying library materials, including trade literature; may be used in combination with other tables.
Notes	In some cases materials have been included with a qualifying adjective, e.g. reinforced concrete. This is intended to reflect common usage within the industry.

Concise Table

P1 Stone, natural and reconstituted

P11 Stone, natural
P12 Stone, reconstituted, reconstructed, cast

P2 Cementitious, concrete and mineral-bound materials

P21 Cementitious materials, binders
P22 Concrete, general
P23 Other mineral-bound materials

P3 Minerals, excluding cementitious

P31 Mineral-based materials
P32 Soils, natural
P33 Clay-based materials
P34 Bitumen-based materials

P4 Metal

P41 Steel
P42 Iron
P43 Aluminium
P44 Copper
P45 Zinc
P46 Lead
P49 Other metals

P5 Timber

P51 Timber, wood, general
P52 Timber, wood, laminated
P53 Timber, wood, fibre building boards

P6 Animal and vegetable materials, excluding timber

P61 Animal, insect material
P62 Vegetable material

P7 Plastics, rubber, chemicals and synthetics

P71 Plastics, general
P72 Plastics, composite
P73 Rubber-based materials, natural
P74 Rubber-based materials, synthetic
P75 Chemicals, synthetics

P9 Combined, other materials, undefined materials

P91 Combined, composite materials
P99 Other materials, undefined

Materials

P1 Stone, natural and reconstituted

P11 Stone, natural
- 01 Basalt
- 02 Bauxite
- 03 Chalk
- 04 Flint
- 05 Granite
- 06 Gravel
- 07 Gritstone
- 08 Limestone
- 09 Marble
- 10 Quartzite
- 11 Sand
- 12 Sandstone
- 13 Slate, natural

P12 Stone, reconstituted, reconstructed, cast
- 1 Slate, composite, reconstituted

P2 Cementitious, concrete and mineral-bound materials

P21 Cementitious materials, binders
- 1 Asbestos cement
- 2 Binders
- 3 Cement
- 4 Fibre cement
- 5 Glass reinforced cement (GRC)
- 6 Mineral fibre cement
- 7 Mortar
- 8 Terrazzo
- 9 Wood wool cement

P22 Concrete, general
- 1 Concrete, aerated
- 2 Concrete, dense
- 3 Concrete, in situ
- 4 Concrete, lightweight aggregate
- 5 Concrete, precast
- 6 Concrete, prestressed
- 7 Concrete, reinforced

P23 Other mineral-bound materials
- 1 Calcium silicate
- 2 Gypsum
  - 1 Glass reinforced gypsum (GRG)
- 3 Lime
- 4 Plaster
- 5 Sandlime

P3 Minerals, excluding cementitious

P31 Mineral-based materials
- 1 Asbestos
- 2 Enamel
- 3 Fired shale
- 4 Glass
  - 1 Glass fibre
  - 2 Glass, cellular
- 5 Mica
- 6 Perlite
- 7 Quartz
- 8 Rock fibre
- 9 Vermiculite

P32 Soils, natural
- 1 Bentonite

P33 Clay-based materials
- 1 Ceramic
  - 1 Glazed ceramic
- 2 Clay
- 3 Earthenware
- 4 Fireclay
  - 1 Glazed fireclay
- 5 Porcelain
- 6 Terracotta
- 7 Vitreous china

P34 Bitumen-based materials
- 1 Asphalt
- 2 Bitumen
  - 1 Bitumen polymer
  - 2 Fibre reinforced bitumen
- 3 Pitch
  - 1 Pitch fibre
  - 2 Pitch polymer

P4 Metal

P41 Steel
- 1 Non-alloy steel, low manganese content
  - 1 Mild steel
  - 2 High-carbon steel
- 2 Non-alloy steel, high manganese content
- 3 Alloy steel
  - 1 Stainless steel
- 4 Coated, protected steel
  - 1 Electroplated steel
  - 2 Galvanised steel
  - 3 Polyester powder coated steel
  - 4 Sherardised steel
  - 5 Sprayed steel
  - 6 Terne coated stainless steel
  - 7 Vitreous enamelled steel
- 5 Steel by purpose
  - 1 Structural
  - 2 For pressure purposes
  - 3 For linepipe
  - 4 Engineering
  - 5 For concrete
  - 6 For rails
  - 7 For cold forming
  - 8 Weathering
  - 9 Corrosion resisting
- 9 Other steels

P42 Iron
- 1 Cast iron
- 2 Malleable iron (spheroidal graphite cast iron)
- 3 Wrought iron

P43 Aluminium
- 1 Aluminium alloy
- 2 Coated, protected aluminium
  - 1 Anodised aluminium
  - 2 Liquid organic coated aluminium
  - 3 Polyester powder coated aluminium
  - 4 Vitreous enamelled aluminium

P44 Copper

P45 Zinc
- 1 Zinc alloy, mazac

P46 Lead

P49 Other metals
- 1 Brass
- 2 Bronze
- 3 Nickel
- 4 Tin
- 5 Tungsten
- 9 Other

Materials

P5	Timber

P51 Timber, wood, general
1 Hardwood
2 Softwood

P52 Timber, wood, laminated
1 Blockboard
2 Glulam
3 Laminboard
4 Plywood
5 Veneers

P53 Timber, wood, fibre building boards
1 Cellulose board
2 Flakeboard
3 Flaxboard
4 Strand board, oriented
5 Waferboard
6 Wood cement particleboard

P6	Animal and vegetable materials, excluding timber

P61 Animal, insect material
1 Hair
2 Leather
3 Silk
4 Wool

P62 Vegetable material
01 Bark
02 Cardboard
03 Coir
04 Cork
05 Cotton
06 Grass
07 Hessian
08 Jute
09 Linen
10 Linoleum
11 Paper
12 Reed
13 Straw

P7	Plastics, rubber, chemicals and synthetics

P71 Plastics, general
01 Acrylonitrile-butadiene-styrene (ABS)
02 Acrylic, polymethyl methacrylate
03 Epoxy
04 Polyamide
   Includes nylon.
05 Phenolic
06 Polycarbonate
07 Polyester
08 Polyethylene, polythene
09 Polyisocyanurate
10 Polypropylene
11 Polystyrene
12 Polyurethane
13 Poly vinyl chloride, plasticised (PVC)
14 Poly vinyl chloride, unplasticised (PVC-U)
15 Urea formaldehyde
16 Vinyl

P72 Plastics, composite
1 Glassfibre reinforced plastic (GRP)
2 Carbon fibre reinforced plastic
3 Resin bonded paper

P73 Rubber-based materials, natural
1 Rubber

P74 Rubber-based materials, synthetic
1 Butyl rubber
2 Neoprene
3 Silicone
4 Polysulfide

P75 Chemicals, synthetics
1 Acids
2 Alkalis
3 Salts

P9	Combined, other materials, undefined materials

P91 Combined, composite materials

P99 Other materials, undefined

Universal Decimal Classification

Examples

Philosophy, mathematics, sport, language, geography, history.

Use

Classifying subjects which are not covered elsewhere in the Uniclass system. For example, Painting (as a fine art), which is classified according to UDC at 75, would be classified at Q75 in the Uniclass system.

As in other sections, class numbers from this section may be combined with another class number using the colon sign. For example D32:Q(44) Offices in France.

Acknowledgement

Universal Decimal Classification (UDC) is an indexing and retrieval language for classifying information on all subjects and in all forms.

UDC is the copyright material of the UDC Consortium, and the English text version is published in the UK by British Standards Institution (BSI). The brief references in this table are based on the International Medium Edition (available from BSI as BS1000M Part 1, Part 2 and Guide to the use of UDC).

Main tables (schedules)

Q0   Generalities

Science and knowledge. Organisation. Information. Documentation. Librarianship. Institutions. Publications

Q00	Fundamentals of knowledge and culture
Q01	Bibliography and bibliographies. Catalogues
Q02	Librarianship
Q030	Encyclopedias. General reference works
Q050	Serial publications. Periodicals (journals, magazines etc.)
Q06	Organisations and other types of cooperation. Associations. Congresses. Exhibitions. Museums
Q070	Newspapers. Journalism. The press
Q08	Polygraphies, Collective works
Q09	Manuscripts, Rare and remarkable works

Q1   Philosophy. Psychology

Q11	Metaphysics
Q13	Philosophy of mind and spirit. Metaphysics of spiritual life
Q14	Philosophical systems and points of view
Q159.9	Psychology
Q16	Logic. Epistemology. Theory of knowledge. Methodology of logic
Q17	Moral philosophy. Ethics. Practical philosophy

Q2   Religion. Theology

Q21	Natural theology. Rational theology. Religious philosophy
Q22	The Bible. Holy scripture
Q23/8	Christianity. The Christian religion
Q23	Dogmatic theology
Q24	Practical theology
Q25	Pastoral theology
Q26	Christian Church in general (nature and character)
Q27	General history of the Christian Church
Q28	Christian churches, sects, denominations
Q29	Non-Christian religions

Q3   Social sciences

Sociology. Statistics. Politics. Economics. Trade. Law. Government. Military affairs. Welfare. Insurance. Education. Folklore

Q30	Theories, methodology and methods in the social sciences. Sociography
Q31	Demography. Sociology. Statistics
Q32	Politics
Q33	Economics. Economic science
Q34	Law. Jurisprudence
Q35	Public administration. Government. Military affairs
Q36	Social work. Social aid. Housing. Insurance
Q37	Education. Teaching. Training. Leisure
Q389	Metrology. Weights and measures
Q39	Ethnology. Ethnography. Customs. Manners. Traditions. Way of life. Folklore

Q4   Vacant

Q5   Mathematics and natural sciences

Q501	Generalities about the pure sciences
Q502	Nature. Nature study and conservation. Nature and wildlife protection
Q504	Environmental science. Environmentology
Q51	Mathematics
Q52	Astronomy. Astrophysics. Space research. Geodesy
Q53	Physics
Q54	Chemistry. Crystallography. Mineralogical sciences
Q55	Earth sciences. Geology. Meteorology etc.
Q56	Palaeontology
Q57	Biological sciences in general. Molecular biology. Virology. Microbiology
Q58	Botany
Q59	Zoology

Q6   Applied sciences. Medicine. Technology

Q60	General questions of the applied sciences
Q61	Medical sciences
Q62	Engineering. Technology in general
Q63	Agriculture and related sciences and techniques. Forestry. Farming. Wildlife exploitation
Q64	Home economics. Domestic science. Housekeeping
Q65	Management and organisation of industry, trade and communication
Q66	Chemical technology. Chemical and related industries
Q67	Various industries, trades and crafts
Q68	Industries, crafts and trades for finished or assembled articles
Q69	Building (construction) trade. Building materials. Building practice and procedure

Q7   The arts. Recreation. Entertainment. Sport

Q71	Physical planning. Regional, town and country planning. Landscapes, parks, gardens
Q72	Architecture
Q73	Plastic arts. Sculpture
Q74	Drawing. Design. Applied arts and crafts
Q75	Painting
Q76	Graphic arts. Graphics
Q77	Photography and similar processes
Q78	Music
Q79	Recreation. Entertainment. Games. Sport

Q8   Language. Linguistics. Literature

Q80	General questions relating to both linguistics and literature. Philology
Q81	Linguistics and languages
Q82	Literature

Q9   Geography. Biography. History

Q902/4	Archaeology. Prehistory. Prehistoric and later remains
Q908	Area studies. Study of a locality
Q91	Geography. Exploration of the Earth and of individual countries. Travel. Regional geography
Q929	Biographical and related studies
Q93/9	History
Q930	Science of history. Ancillary historical sciences
Q931	Ancient history in general
Q94	Mediaeval and modern history (in general)

Common auxiliary tables

Time

From table Ig in BS1000M:1993

Centuries or decades are denoted by 2 or 3 digit notations respectively; e.g.

Q"03"	4th century (300s)
Q"19"	20th century (1900s)
Q"193"	the thirties (1930–39)

Periods embracing several centuries etc. thus:

Q"03/08"	4th to 9th century
Q"1919/ 1939"	the 'inter-war' years
Q"187/ 189"	1870 to 1899
Q"-"	Antiquity BC
Q"+"	Christian Era AD

Place

From table Ie in BS1000M:1993

Q(1)	**Place in general**
Q(2)	**Physiographic designation**
Q(3)	**The ancient world**

Q(4/9)
The modern world

Q(4)	**Europe**
Q(41)	British Isles (geographical whole)
Q(410)	United Kingdom of Gt Britain and N Ireland
Q(410.1)	England
Q(410.3)	Wales
Q(410.5)	Scotland
Q(410.7)	Northern Ireland
Q(415)	Ireland (geographical whole)
Q(417)	Irish Republic (Eire)
Q(430)	Germany
Q(436)	Austria
Q(437.1)	Czech Republic
Q(437.6)	Slovak Republic
Q(438)	Poland
Q(439)	Hungary
Q(44)	France
Q(450)	Italy
Q(460)	Spain
Q(469)	Portugal
Q(47)	Former European USSR
Q(470)	Russia
Q(48)	Scandinavia
Q(480)	Finland
Q(481)	Norway
Q(485)	Sweden
Q(489)	Denmark
Q(492)	Netherlands
Q(493)	Belgium
Q(494)	Switzerland
Q(495)	Greece
Q(497)	Balkan States

Q(5)	**Asia**
Q(510)	China
Q(520)	Japan
Q(53)	Arabia
Q(54)	India, Sri Lanka, Pakistan
Q(55)	Iran (Persia)
Q(56)	South West Asia, Turkey, Cyprus, Iraq, Syria, Lebanon, Israel, Jordan
Q(57)	Former Asiatic USSR
Q(581)	Afghanistan
Q(59)	South East Asia, Burma, Thailand, Malaysia, Cambodia, Vietnam, Laos

Q(6)	**Africa**
Q(61)	Tunisia, Libya
Q(62)	Egypt, Sudan
Q(63)	Ethiopia
Q(64)	Morocco
Q(65)	Algeria
Q(66)	W Africa; e.g. Ghana, Nigeria
Q(67)	Equatorial and Central Africa; e.g. Congo, Uganda, Kenya, Somalia, Tanzania, Mozambique
Q(68)	Southern Africa; e.g. South Africa, Zimbabwe
Q(699)	Islands around Africa

Q(7)	**North and Central America**
Q(71)	Canada
Q(72)	Mexico
Q(728)	Central America
Q(729)	West Indies
Q(73)	USA
Q(74)	N E States
Q(75)	S E States
Q(76)	S Central States
Q(77)	N Central States
Q(78)	W States
Q(79)	Pacific States

Q(8)	**South America**
Q(81)	Brazil
Q(82)	Argentina
Q(83)	Chile
Q(84)	Bolivia
Q(85)	Peru
Q(861)	Columbia
Q(866)	Ecuador
Q(87)	Venezuela
Q(88)	Guiana territories
Q(892)	Paraguay
Q(899)	Uruguay

Q(9)	**South Pacific and Australia. Arctic. Antarctic**
Q(931)	New Zealand
Q(94)	Australia
Q(954)	Papua New Guinea
Q(96)	Polynesia and Micronesia
Q(98/99)	Polar Regions
Q(98)	Arctic territories
Q(99)	Antarctic territories

Index
to the tables

A

B

Babies N5311
Back boilers L75236
Back saws M93117
Backacters M5272
Backhoe loaders M5274
Bacteria N343
Baggage handling facilities at
    airports D1463
Bail hostels D3764
Bains marie L8327
Bakeries D2734
Balconies
    external F332
    internal F331
Balcony units L388
Balers L73232
Baling presses L21744
Ball bearing hinges L418304
Ballast for scaffolding M3271
Ballasts for fluorescent lamps L747364
Ballrooms D5223
Balustrades
    as element for buildings
    – external G251
    – internal G252
    as products L4421
    as work section JL30
Band saws M93124
Bandings L67126
Bandstands D5221
Bank/building society fittings L8581
Banking halls D3391
Banks
    as facilities
    – high street banks D334
    as financial institutions C44121
Banks/dykes L157
Banqueting rooms D5191
Bar cutting/bending equipment M927
Bar reinforcement L3332
Bar sinks L7232
Barbecues L8337
Barbed wire L4431
Barge boards L52941
Bark P6201
Bark roads/pavings JQ23
Barrages
    as facilities D177
    as products L21616
Barrel bolts L418191
Barrel roofs L3822
Barrier trestles M92332
Barriers
    as element for civil engineering
        works H144, H245, H344, H446,
        H545, H645, H745
    as products L44
    – crash L21254
    fire (properties of) N3243
Barrows M936
Bars (licensed premises) D5152
Bars (prestressing) L3342
Bars (reinforcement) L3332
Bars (serving counters) L8341
Barytes L6117
Basalt P1101
Base
    as element for pavements/
        landscaping H121
Base plates M3263
Basement areas F62
Basements F132

Bases
    granular sub-bases for roads/
        pavings JQ20
    in situ concrete JQ21
Bases (military) D3755
Basins L72104
Batch loaders M7255
Batching plant M725
Bath panels L72102
Bath screens L72109
Bathroom cabinets L8241
Bathroom extract fans L75344
Bathroom furniture/fittings L824
Bathroom suites L721
Bathrooms D942
Baths L72101
Batteries L7411
Battery formwork M7421
Baulk timber M331
Bauxite P1102
Bays F122
Bead cavity wall insulation JP11
Beam boxes M2116
Beam shutter clamps M2272
Beams
    for bridges L21102
    precast concrete L3431
    slip finishers for M7424
    timber L362
Beanbags L8716
Bearings for bridges L21109
Bedding L8717
Beddings for coverings/
    claddings L553
Bedpan washers L72332
Bedroom furniture L823
Bedrooms D83
    hotels D858
Beds L8231
Bedside units L8234
Beer gardens D5156
Beetle eradication JC52
Behavioural sciences B94
Belfries D637
Bellframes L84212
Bells L84212
Belt conveyors M451
Belt sanders M93912
Belt weighers M451
Belvederes L22109
Bench grinders M93922
Benches L8225
Benders
    bar M9271
    pipe M9322
Bending strength N3124
Bends for pumps M123
Benefit offices D3153
Bentonite P321
Bentonite clay liners L1415
Bibcocks L725113
Bicycle racks L81103
Bidets L72112
Bills
    priced C686
Bills of quantities C671
Binders P212
Binding agents L62
Binding plant
    concrete block M7435
Bins L8271
    agricultural D2681:E43
Biological attack/damage
    prevention L6818
Biological toilets L721111
Bird baths L81203
Bird boxes L81204

Bird control
    as work section (electronic) JW56
    products for L6862
Birds N342
Bits for drills M9345
Bitumen
    as a general purpose product L625
    as a material P342
Bitumen and fibre profiled sheet
    cladding/covering JH33
Bitumen fibre reinforced thermoplastic
    sheet coverings/flashings JH76
Bitumen trowelled flooring JM12
Bituminous felt shingling JH66
Blackboards L84541
Blackout blinds L4221
Blade hinges L418308
Blankets
    fireproofing L68112
Blast furnace slag L6111
Blast protection film L41862
Blasting equipment M618
Blasting machines M9254
Blinds
    as products L422
    as work section
    – external JL14
Block manufacturing plant M741
Block packaging/binding/shrink foil
    plant M7435
Blockboard
    as a material P5201
    as product L6617
Blockhouses D3756
Blocks as part of a building F11
Blocks of flats/maisonettes D8133
Blocks/blockwork
    as building work section
    – accessories for walling JF30
    – glass JF11
    – interlocking block roads/
        pavings JQ24
    – walling JF10
    as civil engineering work section KU
    as products
    – for fill L122
    – for floors L5332
    – for masonry L322
    – for strip foundations L313
Blood donation/transfusion
    centres D4271
Board cladding JH2
Board sheathings/linings JK2
Boarding M342
Boarding schools D71331
Boards
    fireproofing L68111
    profile (for surveying) M92136
    screed M72323
    thermal insulation L68151
    waterproofing L68131
Boat control facilities D133
Boat storage/repair facilities D1324
Boats for dredging M523
Body care buildings L22107
Body care room units L2223
Body properties and
    characteristics N541
Bogie drop buildings D1173
Boiler houses D16193
Boilers
    as elements G6111
    as products L7521
    as work section JT10
Boiling point N3564
Bollards L81101
    flashing M92335

M

P

PABX systems   L763121
Packaged plant/units
    as element for buildings   G65
    as products
    – air conditioning systems   L75142/3
    – local wet waste treatment   L73171
    – plumbing units   L71111
    as work section
    – steam generators   JT13
Pad foundation products   L311
Padding   L8716
Padlocks   L418185
Pads
    vibration insulation   L68171
Paging systems
    as products   L76114
    as work section   JW11
Paint strippers   L695
Painting
    as building work section   JM60
    – off-site (building fabric reference
        specification)   JZ30
    – off-site (building services reference
        specification)   JY91
    as civil engineering work section   KV
Painting equipment   M935
Paintings   L8734
Paints   L682
    flame retardant   L68115
    intumescent   L68116
Pairs of footprints   M9326
Palaces   D3161
Pallets   M7436
Pamphlets   A93
Panel cladding   JH4
Panel clamps   M2274
Panel pins   L671212
Panel saws   M93115
Panels/panelling
    as products
    – acoustic insulation   L68161
    – ceiling   L542
    – curtain walls   L3811
    – for walls   L5161
    – suspended ceilings   L387
    – tanking   L68141
    – thermal insulation   L68151
    as work section
    – infill   JL42
    – panel partitions   JK30
    – rigid sheet   JK13
    – under purlin/inside rail panel
        linings   JK12
Panic bolts   L418196
Pans for toilets   L721113
Paper   P6211
    resin bonded   P723
Paper lining machines   M74106
Paper manufacturing facilities   D2777
Papers
    decorative   JM52
Parades (buildings)   E824
Paraffin lamps   L7475
Parallel couplers   M32613
Parallelogram type rippers   M52752
Parapets for bridges   L21108
Parcels offices   D1574
Parents   N5321
Park furniture   L812
Parking bollards   L811011
Parking equipment   L2153
Parking facilities
    cars   D125
Parks   D587

Parliament
    European   D3111
    national   D3121
Parliament hinges   L418302
Parquet flooring
    as products   L5332
    as work section   JM42
Partial cutting machines   M6111
Partial mix mortar   L6413
Partially separate sewerage
    systems   D172123
Particleboards
    as material   P536
    as products   L6618
    – hollow core   L6621
Particulate discharge   N3366
Partitions
    as products   L384
    as work section
    – dry   JK3
    – plasterboard   JK10
Partner   C215
Partnering   C44234
Partnerships   C322
    public/private   C332
Parts   N112
Parts for scaffolding   M32
Party wall surveyors   C3834
Passages   F341
Passenger embarkation facilities
    air transport   D1461
    rail transport   D1141
    road transport   D124
    water transport   D1323
Passenger/goods cross-country
    vehicles   M51673
Passengers   N5374
Passing places   D12822
Passive stack ventilation
    systems   L75351
Patent glazing
    as products   L3812
    as work section   JH10
Patent offices   D767
Patents   A261
Pathology facilities   D4171
Patio doors   L411
Patio seating/tables   L81201
Pattern   N1724
Pavement lights
    as products   L415
    as work section   JH14
Pavement recycling machines   M64413
Pavement reshapers   M64412
Pavement rollers   M63181
Pavements (part of road)
    as civil engineering work section   KR
    as entities   E11
    elements for   H1
Pavements (pedestrian)   D12825
Pavilions
    as facilities   D5685
    as products   L22109
Paving stone laying machines   M6418
Pavings
    as products   L534
    as work section   JQ2
    – edgings/accessories   JQ1
Pay and display machines   L21532
Payments
    interim   C7231
Peat cutting facilities   D1673
Pebbledash   L51711
Pedestals
    for museums/galleries   L8443
Pedestrian crossings   D12827
Pedestrian streets   D1231

Pelmets   L87142
Penetration
    of water vapour   N3331
    resistance to mechanical   N3117
Pens
    agricultural   D2685
Pensions   C45911
People   N53
Percussion breakers   M5273
Performance analysis   C8111
Performance properties and
    characteristics   N3
Perimeter
    length of   N15254
Periods/styles of architecture   B13
Perlite
    as material   P316
    as product   L6124
Permanent formwork   L332
Permanent way   D115
Permeability
    to gas/pollutants   N3323
    to water (liquid)   N3343
    to water vapour   N3332
Permission
    planning   C645
Personal financial management   C4425
Personal safety equipment   M9232
Personnel   C2
Personnel management   C45
Petrol interceptors   L21725
Petrol stations   D1261
Petrol/diesel storage/distribution
    systems   JS40
Pews   L84201
PFI   C444413
Pharmaceutical/medical research
    facilities   D73:D4
Pharmacies
    chemists' shops   D3473
    hospitals   D4172
Phenolic   P7105
Photocopying   C4161
Photocopying/computing areas in
    libraries   D7696
Photoelectric cells   L74613
Photograph libraries   D7654
Photographic information   A95
Photographic lighting   L747335
Photographs
    as artworks for interior
        decoration   L8734
    progress   C7243
Photography facilities   D736
Photovoltaic cells   L74216
Physical properties and
    characteristics   N54
Physically handicapped people   N5352
Physiographic properties and
    characteristics   N24
Physiological properties and
    characteristics   N5413
Physiotherapy facilities   D4147
Pick-up trucks   M51672
Picks   M9373
Picture rails/mouldings   L5569
Piers
    as facilities   D1312
    for bridges   H523
Pigeonholes   L863
Piggeries   D2656
Pigtail ties   M2283
Pilasters   L5566
Pile drivers   M622

X

Y

Yards
   agricultural   D2684
   builders'   D2721
Young offenders institutions   D3765
Youth centres   D5341
Youth hostels   D8551

Z

Zinc   P45
Zinc alloy   P451
Zinc sheet coverings/flashings   JH74
Zones   F1
Zoos   D751